naked fruit

D1053312

naked fruit

Getting Honest about the Fruit of the Spirit

Elisa Morgan

Revell

Grand Rapids, Michigan

Published by Fleming H. Revell
a division of Baker Publishing Group
P.O. Box 6287, Grand Rapids, MI 49516-6287
www.revellbooks.com

Third printing, October 2004

Printed in the United States of America

Library of Congress Cataloging-in-Publication Data
Morgan, Elisa, 1955—
    Naked fruit : getting honest about the fruit of the Spirit / Elisa Morgan.
       p.   cm.
    ISBN 0-8007-1873-9 (hardcover)
    1. Fruit of the Spirit. I. Title.
    BV4501.3.M668 2004
    234'.13—dc22   2004011020

Published in association with the literary agency of Alive Communications, Inc., 7680 Goddard Street, Suite 200, Colorado Springs, CO 80920.

To my grand-fruit-of-the-womb

contents

Part 3 Fruit-Filled Living: Getting Honest about Growing a Life That Matters

acknowledgments

Every book comes into being through the partnership of lives. Several people have invested in this project, and it is my privilege to thank them here.

Dr. Haddon Robinson—Thank you for your investment in me over twenty years ago as I originally set much of this material to the tune of *Considerations*, a radio program sponsored by Denver Seminary. Your mentorship in exegesis and communication has carried me through to today.

Cindy Smith—Thank you for your insights on the fruit of the Spirit played out in nearly three decades of a fruit-filled friendship.

Carol Kuykendall—Thank you for holding my hand to the keyboard and for reminding me again and again, "What would a mom need to hear?"

Beth Lagerborg, Beth Jusino, and Stephany Riley—Thanks for reading the manuscript and for offering your "naked" feedback!

Karen Parks—Thanks for the bracelet inscribed with each fruit of the Spirit that I wore as I wrote, manacled to fruit!

Constance Smith—Thanks for making sure I got my fruit "right."

Cyndi Bixler—Thanks for making sure everything was covered while I did the "author" thing.

Rick Christian and Chip MacGregor—Thanks for believing in every idea I come up with and for improving on my ideas with your whittling wisdom.

Jennifer Leep and the staff of Revell—Thanks for this new relationship and for your "naked" courage to launch out with me and with MOPS International!

Evan, Eva, and Ethan Morgan—Thanks for watching me serve, eat, and digest the fruit of the Spirit, not always in such a wonderful way. You teach me what naked fruit looks like in life, and you push me to settle for nothing less as together we grow a life that matters.

introduction

getting past the peeling

Look at the words. Love. Joy. Peace. Patience. Kindness. Goodness. Faithfulness. Gentleness. Self-control.

When we focus on the words—just the words—that compose the classic fruit, we pause. Something stirs inside us. Love? Yes, please! Patience? Absolutely! They're attractive qualities. We *want* them, and we want to reproduce them in our children. We long for them in our days and our nights and in all the moments in between. But how? They seem impossible to grow in our everyday lives, much less in the lives of our little ones. After all, we're not Mother Teresa. We're us. Moms. On the run.

In the trenches. Under stress. Women. Wives, some of us. Daughters making our way. How can we grow such qualities in ourselves or in those we love?

Growing a fruit-filled life of love, joy, peace, patience, kindness, goodness, faithfulness, gentleness, and self-control seems beyond our grasp.

That's because we think that growing such fruit is about being nice. Plus, we think it's all up to us to produce. Neither is true.

It's not about being nice. The truth is that the fruit of the Spirit is about being like Jesus. Jesus was *always* loving, joyful, peaceful, patient, kind, good, faithful, gentle, and self-controlled. But these qualities didn't *always* wear the peeling of "nice" in his interactions. His love was acted out in telling a prostitute to stop sinning and in ordering religious leaders to quit making faith harder than God intended it to be. His kindness led him to touch an outcast leper during a time when such an action was strictly prohibited. His peace put him to sleep in a boat with disciples in the middle of a storm out at sea. Such moments don't define "niceness." But they are definitely fruit-filled. It's not about being nice.

Neither is the fruit of the Spirit all up to us. It's not our job to produce these qualities in our lives or in the lives of those around us. That's God's job: fruit production. The fruit of the Spirit grows when we let him live these qualities in us and through us as we are growing in a relationship with him.

Naked fruit is honest. We don't have to dress it up to make it better. It admits, "I really can't do any more today. I'm bushed. But I'd love to help out tomorrow." It suggests, "A better time for me to commit would be in the early afternoon while the kids are in preschool." Naked fruit isn't 24/7 availability to impossible expectations. But, drawing from a relationship with God, naked fruit does try—openly and sincerely.

Naked fruit is about getting past the peeling of "nice" Christianity and getting down to the honest, simple truth: The fruit of the Spirit is about being like Jesus.

God makes it simple. We make it hard. We want to grow a life that matters, and he wants to grow such a life in us. That's fruit minus the peeling. Naked fruit.

Want a bite?

part one

fruit facts

>>*getting honest about the essentials*

one

fruit i.d.

what is spiritual fruit?

You're in the produce section of your neighborhood grocery store. Just for a minute, lay your list aside and look. Piled high, stacked neatly, and arranged in alternating bands of color are fruits of every imaginable flavor and type. Focus on the fruit.

Apples mirror your reflection in their polished surface. Within their crunchy fruit, seeds make a star-shaped design. Grapefruit exude a tangy, sweet aroma, their skin thick and spongy. Bananas perch delicately, bunched by fives and sixes, yellow skin dotted with brown spots. Strawberries wear their seeds as a cloak. Pineapples guard their syrupy sweetness with a prickly exterior. Coconuts challenge any fruit-eater to break through their barrier to get to the good stuff.

Fruit. Varieties of smells and shapes and sizes. All nutritious. All tasty. Each distinct. Each unique.

Fruit is the result of growth. It's the evidence that a plant or a vine or a tree has been rooted and established, fed and nurtured, watered and staked and pruned to the point of reproducing. Spiritual fruit is what results in our lives when we root ourselves in a relationship with God. When we live a life connected like this with God, he grows his nature in who we are and fruit results: love, joy, peace, patience, kindness, goodness, faithfulness, gentleness, and self-control.

> Spiritual fruit is what results in our lives when we root ourselves in a relationship with God.

Consider the opposite for a moment. In the New Testament, the book of Galatians lists certain qualities resulting from a life disconnected from God. The writer, a follower of God named

Paul, lists putrid produce like "sexual immorality, impurity and debauchery; idolatry and witchcraft, hatred, discord, jealousy, fits of rage, selfish ambition, dissensions, factions and envy; drunkenness, orgies" (Gal. 5:19–21). Not too pretty! Not what we'd paw through at the grocery store! Not what we'd pinch and smell and select to take home to The Fam for the week! Ugh! These are not characteristics we want in our lives.

Ah, but then in verses 22 and 23 Paul describes the results of a life lived in connection with God, a life lived in a healthy direction, a life that makes a difference for tomorrow: "The fruit of the Spirit is love, joy, peace, patience, kindness, goodness, faithfulness, gentleness and self-control."

Precious plums they are! We take in their aroma and our mouths water. They are beautiful to our eyes. We imagine a table spread with their offerings, our families gathered round, plates ready, tummies eager for their sustenance. Here is attractive, appealing fruit that we want in our lives, welcome into the lives of our children, and desire in the lives of those in our world.

The fruits of the Spirit are those God-like qualities that make us look like him. They are his nature exhibited in our personalities. When we plant ourselves in a relationship with Jesus, day in and day out, the result of that relationship is the fruit of his characteristics in us. The fruit of the Spirit is what we look like when we're like Jesus.

For most of us, such a definition comes a bit as a surprise. It can even be unsettling. Looking and acting like Jesus? Huh? Exactly how would that be? That might be a very good thing, but would our own character traits fade away? Would God replace the "me" we know with some saintlike replica that more closely resembles what we believe Jesus to be? Our edgy enthusiasm tamed to a controlled warmth. Our tough determinism melted to a driven discipline. We picture a robotlike woman—only holier. We pull back and wonder, *Will I even recognize myself if I live such a fruit-filled life?* The question haunts, *Will I still be me?*

As I stated in the introduction, the fruit of the Spirit is about more than being nice. Naked fruit gets past the peeling. The fruit of the Spirit is indeed God's characteristics. But it is God's characteristics exhibited in us. Being like Jesus means showing the spirit fruits—as expressed in our own personalities.

"Peace" in your own skin might look like a calm version

of a caffeine addict, whereas in the skin of your neighbor it may look like a lobotomy. "Joy" might appear as stillness in you but more like a whooped-up party in your sister.

For me, this "God's fruit in my own skin" concept comes home when I look at my major life heroes and how far short of their image I fall. Take Mother Teresa. Compassionate. Giving. Fearless. Sacrificial. Content with possessing nothing. I look at the life she lived, immersing herself in the power of Jesus amid poverty and offering hope without ceasing. Wow. Then I look at my whining about how my kids can't seem to keep their junk in their rooms, about how I have to wait in a stack of traffic for an unexpected forty-five minutes while doing errands, about how my husband doesn't move his snack plates from the sink to the dishwasher. Yuk.

> The fruit of the Spirit are those God-like qualities that make us look like him.

Mother Elisa looks very little like Mother Teresa.

But hey, we're so hard on ourselves! Yes, there are way too many moments when ugliness emerges in my life responses. I'm not always nice. But there are actually occasions when I find myself engaged by a friend's need to the point that I race to the hospital to be at her side and don't seem to notice I haven't eaten or even gone to the bathroom for hours. Or I notice a child's favorite shirt is soiled and so throw in an extra load to prepare it for the next day's needs—just cuz I want to help out. Or I notice I'm extra grumpy *before* I lose my tongue and don't actually verbalize what I soooo much want to say.

Maybe I don't look like Mother Teresa all the time. But maybe, just maybe, I look a little bit like Jesus now and then due to the fact that I'm rooted in a relationship with him and he's growing me to be like him.

Wait a minute; I'm saying that it's harder for me to look like Mother Teresa than it is to look like Jesus! Duh, of course. It's always harder for us to repeat the offering of another human than it is to be the best "me" we can be with the help of Jesus.

Love, joy, peace, patience, kindness, goodness, faithfulness, gentleness, and self-control. These are the fruit of the Spirit. These are God's qualities exhibited in our personalities. These are what we look like when we look like God. Strip off the nice and get naked.

Fruit for Thought

1. Think about how peaches grow from a tree, strawberries from a vine, pineapples from a bush. Each fruit looks unique and yet grows as a result of its attachment to the source of growth. Mentally flip through all the people you know who exhibit one or more of the spiritual fruit in their lives: your mother-in-law, your sister, a neighbor, a teacher. Name which spiritual fruits you see in their lives. How does each fruit change from personality to personality? What does this exercise tell you about what spiritual fruit might look like in your personality? Now apply this same thinking to how spiritual fruit might be expressed in your children or in your husband.

2. God's character grows in you as you "plant" yourself in him. Have you ever made such a decision to "plant" yourself in God? Here's how:

> *Dear Jesus,*
> *I want to be like you. I need the help and the promises you offer. I need the hope of being connected to you and*

your perfection in this crazy world. I can't do life by myself without messing it up. Please save me from myself so that I can be the best me I can be by being in a relationship with you. And, as I "plant" myself in you, will you please grow in me these qualities that look like you? I long for a life that matters and that makes a difference in my children, my family, and my world. I realize that happens when these qualities are growing in me out of a relationship with you.

In your name, amen.

The fruit of the Spirit is love, joy, peace, patience, kindness, goodness, faithfulness, gentleness and self-control. Against such things there is no law.

Galatians 5:22–23

two

fruit appetite

*how do we grow a life
that matters?*

You're hungry. You go to the fridge and survey the contents. Milk. Yogurt. Apples. Juice. All the stuff a good mom has on hand for her children but nothing that seems interesting to you: the good mom.

You close the refrigerator door and open the pantry. Chips. Cereal. Dog food. A can of chili. A box of crackers. Nope. Nothing there either.

You're still hungry. Back to the fridge. Ah, leftover mashed potatoes. You warm them in the microwave and down the contents of the container.

Nope. That wasn't it.

Back to the pantry. Ah . . . picante. That'll make the chips tastier. You set out a cup, fill it with the sauce, place it on the center of a plate, and surround it with chips. There. *Crunch. Crunch. Crunch.* The plate empties.

Nope. That wasn't it either. You're still hungry.

So am I. Most of us are. We're hungry for more than what the contents in our fridge can offer. For more than the pantry's holdings. For more than fast food, comfort food, or slow food. We're starving for food that fills, that lasts, that grows something more than just today.

We want fruit.

Huh? Yep. Fruit. Strawberries and cherries and coconuts. Peaches and apples and grapes. We want fruit. Fruit by the foot. Fruit rolled up. Fruit looped about our lives. Fruit as a smoothie for our days. Fruit.

Okay, I'm not whacked. Truly. What I'm talking about is our deep desire to live a life with meaning and to share that meaningful life with others in a way that makes a difference in their days. We want to be more than girls, more than wives, more than moms, even more than women. We want to *matter*, and we want what we do each day to matter as well.

We want our days to be about *more* than the next meal, the next deadline completed, the next errand to the grocery store, the next sale, or even the next girl-time-get-together with our friends. And while it's totally thrilling to watch our child move through each developmental stage—sitting, crawling, walking, talking!—we long for the day when she reads, when she makes her first real friend, when she uncovers her desire to learn, and when she falls in love. We look past today and want to know that what we've invested our time in now will matter tomorrow. We want to leave a legacy with who we are and what we do. We want to grow a life that *matters*.

> We look past today and want to know that what we've invested our time in now will matter tomorrow.

We can. When we eat a diet of fruit and serve up that diet to those around us, we can grow a life that matters.

Love, joy, peace, patience, kindness, goodness, faithfulness, gentleness, and self-control—these make up the fruit of the Spirit, God's fruit grown in us and through us, in his world.

Admittedly, a "diet" of fruit may not appeal to you at first. Suddenly this book feels like the next version of the-diet-you've-always-looked-for books. Magical. Easy. The fix you need. However, as with most diets, you shouldn't expect results overnight.

When I was a child, I didn't like tomatoes. We lived in warm climates where tomatoes grew like dandelions. Tomatoes were a part of most meals. I'd sit down to lunch or dinner—and tomatoes. I'd screw up my face in disgust. In an effort to help me get past my tomato disdain, my mother instituted the Two Bite Rule: "If you take two bites of everything on your plate, one day you'll be big enough to like it." It worked for mashed potatoes. It worked for peas. My mother believed it would work for tomatoes.

I wasn't so sure.

My mom saw my challenge and added an incentive. She pointed across the table to my sister, two years my senior. "Your sister loves tomatoes. See how grown up she is? One day you'll be as mature as she is and you'll like tomatoes too!"

I took the bait. I wanted to be as mature as my sister—absolutely. And so each tomato-accompanied meal, I'd squash down on a cherry globe and wait while the juice oozed over my tongue. I went through a lot of milk, washing down those mouthfuls. Ugh. Gazing at my sister as she swallowed bite after bite, I'd sigh, direct my eyes toward heaven, and prayerfully beg for her maturity, that I too might like tomatoes.

Meal after meal, month after month, two bites of tomatoes, until one day my prayer was answered. I bit down, the juice oozed, my tongue liked it! I liked tomatoes! I checked my flat chest for further evidence of maturity to no avail. Oh well, I was encouraged. At least I liked tomatoes! The rest couldn't be far off! (I have to confess, though, I'm still waiting.)

Two bites a day. We may long for a life that matters, but we aren't too sure about the diet that grows it. We may admire others who model such a life but lack the appetite to dine at their table. However, two bites a day, learning to recognize fruit and bring it to our own refrigerators and pantries and tables, and we'll eventually develop a taste for it.

Love, joy, peace, patience, kindness, goodness, faithful-

> We can live a life that matters by developing a taste for the fruit that will grow it.

ness, gentleness, and self-control. What could possibly matter more than these qualities lived out in our lives and our relationships with others? The result of such naked fruit—unadorned, simple, pure, and true—is a life that is believable, impactful, and purposeful.

We can live a life that matters by developing a taste for the fruit that will grow it.

Fruit for Thought

1. When you were a child, what did you imagine your life would be like as an adult? In other words, what did you want to be when you grew up? How does your life today match up with those dreams?

2. When you look ahead five, ten, even twenty years, what do you want your life to have produced? Think about your life as a wife (if you're married), as a mom, and as a woman. What results do you long for in each area?

3. If you had to chart a course to get you to where you want to go in life, what directions would you give yourself? Would you work on your being, your doing, or both? Where would you place your priorities for the investment of time and money and energy?

4. Of the spiritual fruit listed in the Bible—love, joy, peace, patience, kindness, goodness, faithfulness, gentleness, self-control—which one is most intriguing to you in accomplishing your life goal? Why?

Dear Jesus,

I truly desire to grow a life that matters in myself and in my family. Help me to develop an appetite for spiritual food that will help me accomplish this desire. Shape my "eating habits" to focus on what you want to grow in me.

In your name, amen.

How sweet are your words to my taste,
sweeter than honey to my mouth!

Psalm 119:103

three

fruit markets

what is the purpose of spiritual fruit?

Why does the Bible refer to the qualities of God-likeness as spiritual *fruit*? What's the purpose of this metaphor?

A nursery owner sets out to sell peach trees. She considers approaches. She might peddle pictures of leafy saplings bound in burlap sacks. She might open a four-color catalogue to pictures of peach trees in various seasons of the year: bare branched, flowering, loaded with fruit, and post-fruit. But what really sells a peach tree is the peach it produces—pungent, deep orange, fuzzy skinned, dangling from branches. You can see it. You can smell it. You can touch it. You can taste it. It's the peach that sells the peach tree.

God is the master marketer. He "packages" himself in a wrapper of fruit: love, joy, peace, patience, kindness, goodness, faithfulness, gentleness, and self-control.

Fruit sells God to a world hungry for truth, for hope, and for life.

Fruit markets. Fruit sells God to a world hungry for truth, for hope, and for life. At first that might seem like a bad thing. It's not. Fruit is something we know. We're familiar with these amazing words. God is so much bigger, but he meets us in the language, words, and qualities of our longing so that we might know him.

Fruit is the external result of an internal relationship. Fruit is the dressing that beckons others to know the God we represent. Fruit looks good! It smells good! When we get to know fruit-filled people, we discover that fruit tastes good as well. Like bright oranges standing out against the green leaves of a tree, the fruit of the Spirit announces to a starving world, "Here is food. Here is life. Come and find a way out of exhaustion and discouragement. Come and meet God!"

We want fruit in our lives so much that we desire the kernel of hope that will grow it: God. As a result of our growing relationship with God, we can introduce others to him as well.

My friend Bonnie is a generation above me. Years ago, I met her through my husband's work. More than anyone I can think of, the fruit of Bonnie's life markets the character of God. Dressed daily in love, joy, peace, patience, kindness, goodness, faithfulness, gentleness, and self-control, Bonnie's passion for God is contagious. As a result, she has made me want more and more of God because of the fruit I see in her life.

From the moment Bonnie greets me, whether in person or on the phone, with "Elisa!" I feel loved by God himself. When she asks about the details of my life, I experience an acceptance that demonstrates the deepest kind of patience. From the time they met them as tiny children until now, Bonnie and her husband have sent each of my now-grown children a birthday card carrying a five dollar bill—a kindness my kids have come to count on. And faithful, oh my; Bonnie has been faithful to offer care and prayer through the seasons of my marriage, my mothering, and my life. Bonnie attracts me to the hope I can have in God through the fruit of his character in her life.

One year in particular, I struggled deeply with my relationship with my mother. I grew up in a "broken" home. My parents divorced when I was five, and my mother—bless her heart—battled alcoholism all the years of her adult life. While she knew God as a young child, she refused him in her adult days. In my thirties, my personal work included healing from the confusion of my childhood and specifically, a very codependent relationship with my mother. I had been more of a mother to her than she had been to me.

When I learned that my mother had cancer, instead of feeling the conclusion of our mother/daughter journey, I experienced panic; I thought I was responsible for her eternity. I found myself hopeless, loveless, and prayerless.

So I turned to Bonnie. I asked Bonnie to pray for my mother because I couldn't. She did. Daily. Faithfully.

From time to time she'd check in and ask me for topics, words, or concerns. What did I want her to pray for my mother? I told her to please pray that my mother would see her need for God and that she would desire heaven. I waited. Bonnie prayed.

The week my mother died, she called to tell me that she'd remembered two poems, both spiritual in nature. One was "L'Envoi" by Rudyard Kipling—all about heaven. The other was "Footprints in the Sand." At last. My mother had come to see her need for God and had begun to desire heaven.

Bonnie's fruit-filled prayers have kept God before me, guiding me to him and to the fruit he longs to grow in my life. See—fruit in one life "markets" the hope of Jesus to another life.

I'm not the only one who needs an up-close-and-personal example of fruit-filled living to grasp how fruit would look in my life. We all ask the questions: How does patience work with a cranky toddler? Where does a sweet voice come from when it's a struggle just to stay calm? Will we still grow the fruit of kindness if we say no to distractions in order to get things done? How? We look at others and want real help. Others look at us and want the same, not some "nice" version of faith that they can never hope to have. Seeing the patience, the faithfulness, the gentleness of Jesus in the life of a Christian, others outside the faith are attracted to God. They reach and grab for the promise offered by naked fruit, hungry for the message it sells.

Fruit draws people to God and the hope they can find in him.

Fruit markets. Fruit draws people to God and the hope they can find in him. Love. Joy. Peace. Patience. Kindness. Goodness. Faithfulness. Gentleness. Self-control. Wrap up your life in these qualities and let God offer his character through you to the hungry in the world around you.

Oh—one more thing. Resist the urge to glitz, spin, and alter your life's advertisement for Jesus. The fruit of the Spirit is wrapper enough for the truth of God's character extended to us. We tend to think, *Oh, it's up to me to make God look good! I must improve his image before others! It's my job to clear up the confusion out there about who God is!* Sometimes we're tempted to plaster on a smile on a non-smiley face, hoping to portray an image of joy. Or gloss over the inevitable pain of life when a friend contracts cancer. Or guarantee a happy life in exchange for a child's faithful trust in Jesus. While "spinning" the truth is an acceptable practice in advertising, we're wise to avoid this practice in fruit marketing.

Think naked fruit. Just fruit. That's how God intended nature to reveal his being, and that's how he wants us to represent him as well. Naked fruit—simple, pure, and truthful—is advertisement enough: love, joy, peace, patience, kindness, goodness, faithfulness, gentleness, and self-control.

Spiritual fruit is fruit with a spiritual purpose. Naked fruit markets God to a world hungry for the hope they can have in him.

Fruit for Thought

1. Go get an apple, a peach, or a lemon from the fridge or out of the fruit bowl on your kitchen counter. Cut it open and look at its parts. Skin. Body. Seed. Depending on your selection, what lessons can you learn from the physical qualities of this fruit?

2. Now think back on someone you know whom you respect for how they seem to know God. What qualities drew you to this person at first? How, like fruit, did such characteristics attract you to want more of what they possess?

3. Love. Joy. Peace. Patience. Kindness. Goodness. Faithfulness. Gentleness. Self-control. Let your eye scan this list while asking yourself, Which of these fruits do my children need to see in my life in order to see the God I love? Which one does my husband need to see as an advertisement of the hope I have in God? What about a friend at work—which fruit in your life might "market" God's love to her?

4. Think back to the point about "spinning" in advertising. Are there ways in which you've decided that it's up to you to handle how God looks to others—improving or protecting his reputation? When you realize that he is best seen in the fruit of the Spirit as expressed in your personality, where do you sense the need to peel off the unnecessary outsides of your life and get down to the naked fruit?

Dear Jesus,

I am changed by the understanding that the purpose of your fruit is to draw others to the hope and help they can have in you. I also realize that I'm sometimes tempted to add on to your clear qualities and probably end up muddying your image rather than modeling it. Help me to relax in who you really are and let you grow these fruits of your character purely and simply in my days without embellishment, trusting you with the results.

In your name, amen.

Clothe yourselves with the Lord Jesus Christ.

Romans 13:14

four

fruit maturity

how do we get growing?

Back in my mother-of-preschoolers days I used to count the minutes until I could plop down on the couch with my two cherubs and zone out in front of *Sesame Street*. After hours of getting kids in and out of car seats, cutting up sandwiches into bite-sized morsels, lap-reading, and nose-wiping, I finally rested.

I remember an episode in which Telly Monster had surrounded himself with all kinds of healthy foods. In between bites of carrot, Telly stretched and groaned, urging his pudgy body upward. When asked what he was doing, Telly replied, "I'm trying to grow!"

I relate to Telly Monster. I'm one of those petite-type women who never really bloomed past fifth grade. In fifth grade I was a giant at five feet two inches. I wore a size five and a half shoe. I towered over the boys, yet to come to their prime. I can remember focusing on eating healthy and exercising, but every time I backed up against the doorjamb where I'd marked my height, the measurement remained unchanged.

Today I measure a half shoe size larger and one inch taller (must have been all those doughnuts in college). There really wasn't much I could do to change my genetic makeup of height and shoe size.

While there are certainly moments when I'm stunned that I'm the mom (You mean *I* have to figure out what's for dinner *every* night?) and I'd rather remain childlike in my responsibilities (Can't someone else pay this bill for me?), in general I *want* to grow in all areas of my life. You too, no doubt. I mean, it's as if we were *born* to grow. We're propelled forward. There's something exhilarating about getting your driver's license, learning to navigate a new city after a move, sharing your thoughts in a book club, mastering Outlook on the computer, completing an entire dinner with side dishes and getting it on the table—hot. Growing is good.

But what role do *we* play in growing God's good fruit in our lives? Love, joy, peace, patience, kindness, goodness, faithfulness, gentleness, and self-control. Eat and exercise and measure as we may, our efforts produce about as much as the efforts of Telly Monster on *Sesame Street* and me in fifth grade.

Here's why. Our genetics determine the results of our physical bodies. We can influence the outcome with our efforts, but in the end, what we look like—height, shoe size, eye color—is up to how we're designed. Similarly, while we have a role in the growing process, our spiritual growth is up to God.

> While we have a role in the growing process, our spiritual growth is up to God.

When we receive the seed of hope into the soil of our lives and begin a connected relationship with God, he lives inside us. We get his spiritual DNA. Like a twenty-four-hour-a-day gardener, God tills the soil of our lives until we begin to grow qualities that resemble his nature. By his interest and effort in us, we grow into holy orchards.

Only God can reproduce his nature in us.

By our own efforts, based on our own natures, we'll grow fruit of the flesh. It might be nice, but it won't look like Jesus. It won't be naked fruit. Our best efforts won't grow godliness, because the fruit of the Spirit comes forth only from godly seeds. We can't make ourselves look like God. Only God can do that. Only God can reproduce his nature in us.

Make sense?

But that's not all. With all this said, we do have a role in our growth. Just as we can't grow spiritual fruit without God, God can't grow spiritual fruit in us without us.

Our job in spiritual growth is to cooperate with the Gardener.

Here's what cooperation looks like in our lives.

First, *we're receptive*. A seed can't get into hard, clay-packed soil. Our job includes staying soft so that we can receive the seeds God wants to plant in our lives. Admittedly, being receptive can be a challenge at times. We defend against the seeming intrusion of another's agenda. What if we're not in the mood for God to grow us? What if we'd rather slump down on the couch in front of *ER*? What if we *like* the dullness of our days because there's a kind of predictable safeness there?

When we recognize such resistance, we're wise to tell a friend, say a prayer, or just gently remind ourselves that God's not out to get us with his fruit. He simply wants us to grow the way we want ourselves to grow: into people who make a difference and live lives that matter.

Second, *we endure pruning*. Part of the growing process involves cutting off what is diseased or no longer necessary or even what is taking nutrients that are needed elsewhere.

Yikes. If you ask me, it's much harder to endure pruning than to be receptive to new growth. Pruning can be painful! We don't want to part with some stuff that may actually need to go. Sarcasm is fun! Oh, it isn't being like Jesus? Hmm. Grudges? Oooh, but they're so self-vindicating! Oh, they're not like Jesus.

You get the point. Someone has said, "You're not in a growth zone if you're in a comfort zone, and you're not in a comfort zone if you're in a growth zone." Ouch.

The third way we cooperate is *we stay connected*. We can't grow spiritually if we detach from the source of our growth. A leaf doesn't continue growing once it's pulled from a branch. When we stop hanging out with others who care about growing, we'll probably stop growing too. When we let week after week slip by without going to a church service or a study group or even spending some time opening up ourselves to God in prayer, we'll shrink rather than grow.

Ready to get growing? It's up to God to grow his fruit in our lives, but it's up to us to cooperate with him. Just as we can't grow spiritual fruit without God, God can't grow fruit in us without us.

Fruit for Thought

1. In what ways is God growing the fruit of his nature in your life? What is he "doing" to develop his characteristics in your personality?
2. How can you cooperate more with the Gardener who wants to help you grow? In what area are you resisting rather than receiving? Where might you

be resisting rather than enduring his pruning? And how is it difficult for you to stay connected?

> *Dear Jesus,*
>
> *Thank you that growing in these qualities is a two-way, mutual process. You don't ask that I lay down who I am and become robotic in my responses. Instead, you invite me to join your work in me and through me in the world. I choose to cooperate.*
>
> *In your name, amen.*

Other seed fell on good soil. It came up and yielded a crop, a hundred times more than was sown.

Luke 8:8

part two

naked fruit

>>*getting honest about* . . .

five

love

being there . . . in everything

The quality of a grape is directly related to its host vine. Grapes abide in their vine. Detached from their source, they wither. Grapes offer an example of commitment through the easy and hard times of life. In fact, vine growers report that the sweetest grapes come from the most stressed vines.

Love. Joy. Peace. Patience. Kindness. Goodness. Faithfulness. Gentleness. Self-control.

First on the list: love. Easy, right?

Take marriage. The early months and years are ecstatic!

Every glance satisfies. Every exchange rewards. And surely, in many, many marriages, such "magic" remains long into advanced seasons, developing into a mature and mutual love.

How about motherhood? Our initiation is glorious! No matter how wrinkly, red, or ridiculous our baby might appear to others, to us he or she is spectacular! Amazing! No duration of labor or surgery or fear of the unknown could hold our hearts back from the complete delight of loving this little child who has become ours through birth or adoption.

Among all the qualities of God's character produced in us by his Spirit, love seems the most natural, second nature, and easiest to both offer and receive.

Until some unexpected evening when our darling husband calls, late for the millionth time on the very night we've scheduled dinner with a girlfriend and we're utterly dependent upon him to take over so we can take off. In that moment our previously unending sense of love evaporates like water off a car hood on a hot summer afternoon.

Or until that precious baby whimpers to a full-blown howl at 3:00 in the morning and there is no one to take a turn besides us because the man we love is traveling . . . or never stayed around long enough to sign up fully for fatherhood. Oh, we love that baby more than our own life, but the desire for sleep seduces us into a rage that tug-of-wars our attention away from our child and the love we'd purposed to extend.

Love. Indeed, seemingly the easiest of all qualities to model in so very many moments. Love is there . . . in all things. Except when love is hard. And it can be hard, can't it?

Let's get real (naked!) about love. It can be *hard* to love people. Love means handing over the remote control when we'd rather keep it, getting up just when we're all settled in a comfy spot, speaking in a balanced tone of voice when we'd rather scream, opening our heart to listen to another when we'd rather allow our own feelings to tumble out. Yep, it's hard to love people.

Besides that, *people* can be hard to love. Baby people we once carried in our own bodies. Children people we desired more than life itself. Husband people we're married to. Parent people we've called Mom and Dad for our entire lives. Neighbor people we live next to. Friend people we invite over for dinner. They all seem to want what we don't always want to give—and when we're not in the mood to give it. When we do go out of our way to love, sometimes they're grateful and appreciative and reciprocate. But there are also moments when people are picky and critical and snippy, and we wonder why we bother trying. People are hard to love.

> Love is not about being nice for the sake of niceness; it's about being like Jesus.

How can we grow this fruit of love in our lives and in the lives of others—in *everything*? It's not a big deal to love when it's easy, but when it's hard, then what? Are we to plaster on the martyr mom mask and grit our way through? Should we smile submissively and pretend to love the man we're so very ticked at? Is that what love looks like—nice, nice, nice all the time even when it's hard?

Love is not about being nice for the sake of niceness; it's about being like Jesus. What would Jesus do in the everyday when it's hard to love hard-to-love people?

I've been married for twenty-five years. In the early years of my marriage—and before, when we were dating—I thought love meant anticipating each other's every need and rushing in to fix it before something was even broken. I thought love meant feeling the same way about political issues, personalities, and what time to turn off the lights at night. I couldn't imagine arguments as a part of a loving relationship, or selfishness seeping into whose turn it was to go to the store, or judgment layered over discipline dealt out to children.

Was I ever wrong!

In real life, twenty-five years and two children later, it's clear to me that, indeed, all this confusing stuff does fit into the world where love lives. Choosing a commitment to love in the "everything" of such skirmishes teaches us that love can coexist with conflict and even grow stronger through it.

Similarly, I imagined that motherhood would produce Elisa-cloned children who hold my views, make the choices I would make, and express emotions I feel. Not. Instead, I'm finding real individual children who are growing into real individual adults, unique and distinct from my definition and me. Choosing a commitment to my children, I find my heart growing a love I didn't realize was possible, shaped by the challenges and deepened through diversity.

Love is a committed choice to be there . . . in everything.

An example of love up close and personal comes from our family hamster. Yep, a hamster. It was about 9:30 one night when my daughter, Eva, then about thirteen, shrieked at me from her bedroom down the hall.

> Love is a committed choice to be there . . . in everything.

"Mom!!! Come here! Now!!!!"

I ran in response to find my daughter standing rigidly above her hamster's cage, eyes wide and mouth agape. "BeeBee's having babies!" she announced.

Sure enough, seven-week-old BeeBee, an occupant in our home for only two weeks, was a mother. Eleven (did you get that—*eleven?*) half-inch-long worm-like babies were mouthing the air about her, searching for food. *Ahhh,* I thought, *bless your heart, BeeBee.*

In the days that followed, BeeBee ate—that she might feed her babies. She slept, sprawled out for her babies to reach—that she might warm her babies. She shoved pine straw in womblike piles—that she might protect her babies. One morning we peeled back the towel that covered the cage to find it empty. Gasping, I searched for the itty-bitty babies. I pictured *National Geographic* moments in which wild animals eat their young, and I panicked with worries of what BeeBee had consumed for breakfast.

At last I discovered BeeBee with her brood, safely snuggled inside her plastic hamster ball. She had scooped them all in with her and sat happily feeding all eleven. As I peered down at her, she dislodged herself from her spot and struggled through the ball's opening to greet me, dragging eleven mouths along.

"Oh, BeeBee!" I whispered. "You're doing such a good job!" This was choice. This was commitment. Motherhood. Love: a committed choice to be there . . . in everything.

When it's hard to love hard-to-love people, the fruit of love helps us in the "everything" moments of life. As God is the source of all the spiritual fruits, he is the source of love. Because he loves us in the "everything" of life, we can love others. He shows us the way.

In the "everything" moments, love is a *choice*. God chose to love us. He didn't have to. He wanted to love us, so he chose to love us. We *choose* to love others. Sure, sometimes it doesn't seem like a choice, like when we fall in love with our baby, our husband, or even a best friend. That's more of a "can't help but feel it" emotion, isn't it? But later, when the newness of love wears off and we're caught in a relationship, it is the *choice* of love that continues. And when we

> **Love is a commitment to keep choosing to love . . . even when you don't feel like it.**

find ourselves in relationships we haven't "chosen"—neighbors, in-laws, and co-workers—love wakes up and chooses all over again, intentionally this time.

Love is also *commitment*—in everything. God is committed to us, no matter what. Love stays when it wants to go. It accepts when it wants to reject. It does what it doesn't want to do when it doesn't want to do it. It gets above the "can't stand this person" moments and, squinting, forces itself to look at that someone the way God looks at them, seeing them flawed, yes, but filled with potential. Love is a commitment to keep choosing to love . . . even when you don't feel like it.

And thus, God-like (BeeBee-like, if you will), we choose, we commit to, and we *practice* this kind of love in "everything" and get better at it bit by bit. Notice I didn't say perfect. We won't ever be perfect at loving. But we can be better. More honest in our love. More consistent. More expressive. Quicker. When we give a back rub, mail a note of encouragement to a friend, plant a smooch on the cheek of our kindergartener, or wash the communion cups at church, we are practicing love. What we practice we improve.

In many life moments, love comes easily. But when love is hard, we're helped by recalling what love is: a committed choice to be there . . . in everything. Love is the fruit that gets us past the "being nice" part of politeness to the naked offering of love when it's hard to love hard-to-love people.

Fruit for Thought

1. When is it most difficult for you to love someone? Try to be specific about what circumstances might trigger your resistance. Fatigue? Woundedness? When you don't feel safe? When life seems unfair? Pinpoint what might be holding you back from both receiving and giving love in your life.

2. Name someone who is hard for you to love. Can you pinpoint what is hard to love about this individual?

3. What do you think God sees when he looks at this person? Does God choose, and commit, and practice this committed choice in his love for this person? How do you know this to be true?

4. Think about how you might be "working up your own love" for this person rather than allowing Jesus to love them through you. What does such effort produce in you? As Dr. Phil says, "How's that working for you?" Okay, how can you shift the "source" of your love from yourself to God by letting Jesus love that person through you?

5. Is there a spot in your life where you are loving too much? A relationship that defines you, imprisons you, controls you? Step back and reevaluate what love really requires of you in this relationship and where you might be responding to what isn't love at all.

6. Take a few moments to think through what you know about this hard-to-love person until you come up with three characteristics you like/admire/enjoy. Now take these characteristics and choose, commit

to, and practice that choice to be there in everything by praying this prayer:

Dear Jesus,

I offer up _____ and ask that you would help me to love him/her. I see that I have difficulty loving when I'm _____ and/or _____. I can identify _____, _____, and _____ as characteristics I like/admire/enjoy in this person. Please help me to see these qualities each time I'm with this person, and from this beginning, please grow your love for them within me. Help me to see them the way you see them and to love them the way you love them.

In your name, amen.

Love is patient, love is kind. It does not envy, it does not boast, it is not proud. It is not rude, it is not self-seeking, it is not easily angered, it keeps no record of wrongs. Love does not delight in evil but rejoices with the truth. It always protects, always trusts, always hopes, always perseveres. Love never fails.

1 Corinthians 13:4–8

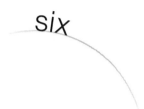

six

joy

having confidence in God

In one juicy, tangy bite, the cherry offers its splendor. But watch out! Before swallowing its delicious meat, you must discard the pit.

Joy and happiness. What's the difference?

Happiness comes from the root *hap*, which means chance. Happiness is circumstantial. It has to do with life going the way we want it to go and the feeling we experience when that happens. Like a Christmas morning when your favorite relatives are present, everyone likes their gifts, and the baby cooperates with your predetermined schedule. Like a perfect wedding day when the sun shines, the flower girls behave, and the groom remembers what really matters as you appear at the end of the aisle. Like the birth of a healthy baby born to a couple who love each other and are committed to the every day and every night of parenthood together.

Happiness. It's a good feeling based on good circumstances. No doubt, happiness is something to enjoy and celebrate on those occasions when it *happens*. But there are so many other moments in life when life doesn't *happen* according to our desires!

What then? What can we expect to experience when life turns upside down, when we get nothing we want and everything we don't want?

Ah . . . that's the opportunity for joy!

Where happiness is circumstantial, joy is not. Joy is more than happiness. The Old Testament describes joy as a quality of life as well as an emotion. The spontaneous songs of worship contained in the Psalms illustrate this kind of joy. Joy is something deep that celebrates God's character despite the circumstances. Shouts of joy after a lengthy battle. Joy that comes in the morning after a night of mourning. Garments of joy that replace sackcloth.

In the New Testament, joy is often expressed as ecstasy, a feeling of amazement, an uninhibited response to God's grace and presence in our days—like the tidings of "joy" brought to the shepherds by the angels at the birth of Christ. Joy is also connected to hope, to love, and to a perspective that sees beyond the immediate to the eventual as New Testament writers look toward the resolution of their anguish and toward heaven.

When all the roots are uncovered and all the meanings parsed and defined, the Bible offers an overall definition of this elusive quality. To be honest, it surprises me. The fruit of joy is confidence in God. Joy is confidence in God's grace, despite circumstances—despite what *happens.* Joy is the ability to hold up because we know we are being held up. Joy is the conviction that God is in control of every detail of our lives even when those details appear to be out of control.

Joy comes on a Christmas morning spent with un-

> Joy is the ability to hold up because we know we are being held up.

favorite relatives who gripe about their gifts. It boldly turns its gaze to the reason behind the celebration and, remembering this, inhales with deep confidence.

Joy comes to a rainy wedding day with grumpy flower girls who stubbornly plop down mid-aisle, refusing to budge, so the bride is forced to pick her way around the pile of tulle to reach her groom. Fueled by a love that recognizes "in sickness and in health, in wealth and in poverty," joy welcomes the "whatever" of this sacred celebration.

Joy rises up out of cascading fear when a baby doesn't breathe in the first moments after delivery. With eyes searching a spouse for hope and hands reaching out for proof of life, joy swallows terror and resolves that this little life is being held by hands larger and more capable than those of a mother, a father, or even a doctor.

Joy is confidence in God no matter what *happens*.

Joy is confidence in God no matter what *happens*. Because we've watched God working in so many moments of life—good, bad, confusing, sorrowful, challenging, unfathomable—when we are joyful, we are wrapped up by our observations and held in place, knowing clearly that just as God came through before, he will come through again.

Joy has a way of buoying us up in the midst of the unpredictable. We're somehow hopeful. Strong. Clear. Confident. We still wonder. We still worry. We still cry and fear and yearn. But beneath all these feelings is the comforting thought that we are held in God's hands.

How can we absorb such a concept of joy when we've tasted only lightly of life's terrors? When we are mothers who still idealistically believe we can stand between pain and our child, between disappointment and our daughter, between tragedy and our son? When we are women bent on creating a safe world for those we love, a cocoon of predictable provision?

Perhaps we can't completely. But maybe by taking small steps toward joy in our early parenting days, we can develop a recognition of this fruit and our need for it as life's steps steepen.

When I discovered that my fourth-grade daughter had a learning disability, joy was the reassurance that God already knew this and that he knew what it would mean for her.

When I was told that my mother had cancer, joy was

the security that the days of her life were numbered before she even came to be.

Today, when I realize there are moments I can't protect my children from all the dangers of this world, joy is the security that God is present all the time, even in my absence in their lives. They will walk where I cannot go. But wherever they go, God is already present.

At five, my son, Ethan, began to teach me this lesson. We'd had a busy morning. The cleaners. Then the library. The hair salon. Finally, the grocery store.

Arriving home, we unloaded the car from our morning of errands and all the paraphernalia Ethan utilized to occupy himself while we were out and about. On errand days, he always armed himself with piles of entertainment for the "just in case I get bored" moments that might arise. Plopping his stash down on the couch, he began to pick through the pile while I put away groceries.

"Mom! My binoculars! They're not here!" a voice of alarm leap-frogged over the half-wall separating family room from kitchen. Yikes. We'd been to tons of places. In and out of the car. To and from stores. Perhaps he'd mislaid them here at home and hadn't taken them along.

Ethan seemed positive he'd put them in his backpack and had played with them at some errand stop. Just to be sure, we split up and scoured the house. I looked under beds and couches and in closets. He inspected his room. We met on the stair landing, empty-handed. I couldn't think of anywhere else to search. Looking into his furrowed face, I was worried. "Ethan, I don't know where else to look! I think they're lost." I reached down, offering comfort.

Ethan studied my face. "Mom, we may not know where they are, but Jesus does. Why don't we just ask him?" he asked.

Amazing. On the stair landing, I followed my son's lead and bowed my head. We acknowledged that Jesus knew where Ethan's binoculars were. We asked him to show us. Then we got back in the car, fastened our seat belts, backed out of the garage, and retraced our steps through our morning errands. Back to the cleaners. The library. At the hair salon, the receptionist welcomed us warmly, holding up a pair of very familiar binoculars. "Are you here for these?" she questioned. "I found them under a chair and remembered Ethan playing with them. I figured you'd know where you left them, and I was just waiting for you to be back to fetch them!"

Ethan embraced his binoculars and winked up at me. "Well, we didn't know *exactly* where they were, but we knew someone else did and that he'd show us!"

It was a simple lesson in joy, taught to me by a five-year-old innocent boy who had barely scraped his knee on the barbed wire of life. Looking back, that moment stands as a testimony of confidence in God no matter what *happens*.

I don't really want to pop the bubble of hope provided by youth, or newness, or even denial. But I do know—from falling myself and from being caught in the grasp of a God I can't escape—life is unpredictable and contains many unpleasant moments that *happen*. And when they do, joy is the experience of holding on because we know that we are being held.

Naked joy is vulnerable. Honestly, it's not the nice version of life we thought we signed up for. It's not about us getting what we want when we want it. It's about God and his character—and what we really believe about him. Such joy is more than the happiness that *happens* when life *happens* to go the way we want. Naked joy reveals to us what we believe about God. Further, it reveals what we believe about God to those who are watching and wondering how we'll respond when life *happens* to let us down.

Fruit for Thought

1. When we observe joy in others—a solid confidence in God's character that the normal and even sensational bumps of life don't alter—we are impressed. We find ourselves drawn to know the God who can produce such a state in mere mortals. Think about your family and friends. Who exhibits the kind of joy we've been talking about in this chapter? What does their example do to your heart?

2. The philosopher Nietzsche once said, "I would believe in their salvation if they looked a little more like people who have been saved." Do you look like you've been "saved"? What would joy look like in your personality? In your particular circumstances today?

3. Several years ago, people used this acronym for joy:

J: Jesus First

O: Others Second

Y: Yourself Last

What do you think of such a definition? What could be helpful from this mantra as you live a life of joy and as you teach your children to do so? What might be the inherent dangers of such an attitude?

4. The Bible often encourages us to "rejoice in the Lord." What does it mean to put the word *joy*, a noun, into verb form? How do we *do* joy? Or how do we *joy* in our lives?

> *Dear Jesus,*
>
> *Naked joy is a bit scary. It's facing the good and the bad of life with you, knowing that you are God in all. Help me to courageously put my confidence in you today so that no matter what happens tomorrow I will be able to experience the joy of knowing you are in control of both.*
>
> *In your name, amen.*

Consider it pure joy, my brothers, whenever you face trials of many kinds.

James 1:2

seven

peace

resting in God

The blueberry is a heart-healthy fruit, providing the largest fruit source of antioxidants that prevent cancer and other diseases as well as possessing antiaging and anti-infection properties. Blueberries reduce the results of stress in our lives.

Typically we think of peace as the absence of irritation. A quiet afternoon composed of naptime for the kids and a cup of coffee with a good read for us. No phone calls. No early awakenings. No to-do list.

Surprise! The fruit listed in Galatians 5 conveys something different than our view of peace. It's less about real life lining up according to our desires and more about our desires lining up to real life.

After the end of the Vietnam War, the American Art Institute hosted a contest requesting the submission of artistic expressions of the meaning of peace. Hundreds of entries poured in, many depicting a somewhat stereotypical view of tranquility—beach scenes at sunset, mountain streams, wide valleys framed by hills.

The institute surprised participants and the press with their selection of a winner. Rather than the best of the best of these tranquil portrayals, an unusual painting was decreed the most accurate expression of peace.

Picture this: a raging storm—wild and tumultuous. Standing before its whirl, you can feel wet spray blow across your cheeks. Thunder rumbles in your bones, reverberating through your body. In the middle of the picture is an open field where a solitary tree stands against the howling wind, bowed by its strength. Tucked into a branch in the tree is a nest where a mother bird cups her babies in safety. This bird has built a nest of rest for herself and for her family. In it she hides, secure and calm in the middle of the storm. A one-word title captured the painting's offering: *Peace*.

The book of Mark describes a scene much like this painting. The disciples were on the Sea of Galilee, with Jesus in the boat asleep, when a wild storm came up. As the waves broke over the boat, threatening to sink it, they cried in terror to their sleeping Teacher, "Don't you care if we drown?" At this, Jesus got up, rebuked the wind and the waves, and questioned the disciples as to their lack of faith.

Peace is the result of resting in God. Peace comes from resting in a relationship that holds us in the midst of life's storms *and* in the momentary calm of their aftermath.

> Peace is the result of resting in God.

Sleeping through the storm, Jesus exemplified the true meaning of peace that arises from rest. Jesus rested in the boat because he rested in his relationship with his Father. Completely convinced of God's control over the externals, Jesus was able to relax to the point of sleep.

Rest? How does that work for a mom? Rest is a four-letter word to most of us—an impossibility we take on our tongue and then spit out in frustration when we don't get it! We race from car pool to dentist to meeting to market. Beckoned by the washer, whiny children, and the weekend's activities, we march according to the orders of others. Rest? When? How? It's funny how a good thing like rest can send us into a tailspin of effort. It feels so "all up to us" to manufacture, doesn't it? If we had more faith, more patience, more laid-backness, wouldn't we be more restful and therefore more peaceful? Silly us! We attack the subject of rest with an itinerary that spells DO IT! and end up undoing the very result we're after.

> **Rest restores our souls.**

The Chinese pictograph for *busy* is made up of two characters: *heart* and *killing*. Busyness kills our hearts. Rest restores our souls. The naked fruit of peace comes when we peel away the *killing* and focus instead on the *heart* of living. That means our relationship with God.

Author Henry Blackaby tells of a time when he planned to visit a farmer on his land. He called ahead for directions and received a blurry commentary containing the exact number of fence posts, certain colors of silos, and the direction of ditches he must follow. Henry carefully followed the instructions and made it to the farm but reported that tension and anxiety accompanied him throughout the journey.

His next trip to the farm was different—and not just because it was his second time around. He drove easily, completely relaxed and peaceful, because the farmer himself was his passenger along the way. Henry merely had to take directions from his companion—turn right at the silo; keep it at no more than thirty; up ahead at the stand of trees, veer to the left—and he arrived safely. He rested in the relationship with his friend and experienced a kind of peace as he traveled.

Peace is the result of resting in a relationship with God.

Whew.

How, like a little bird in a howling storm, do you need to build a nest of rest in a relationship? Where can you simply lay down the busyness and meet life with a more openhanded stance that receives whatever it brings you? Peace can come in the middle of an up-in-the-middle-of-the-night-with-a-sick-child trauma. During the day when the dog and the phone and the toddler all ring out their needs around you. While you're caught up late in a meeting and unable to get where you need to go. Peace can come in all these circumstances because peace comes in a relationship with a God who is with us in such stormy moments.

Naked peace peels away the "nice" expectation that we'll feel calm in the absence of irritation and instead embraces the calm that comes from resting in the midst of it.

Fruit for Thought

1. Still not sure what it might look like to find peace resulting from rest in real life? Imagine a scene in an airport. You are traveling alone with two children under four. Understandably, you're a bit nervous, but when you hear the announcement that the plane is delayed due to weather, the small kink in your stomach becomes a twisting knot. You review the contents of your carry-on and worry that you don't have enough reserves for a long layover.

   Now, lean back into this truth: You are not alone. God is with you. Rest in your relationship with him. What instructions might he offer? Go to the newsstand and replenish? Don't fret; you've packed enough already?

In the "dailiest" moments, you can practice the presence of God by remembering that peace is the result of resting in a relationship with a real God who is really there.

2. Stereotypes of peace can get in the way of experiencing this fruit. Make a mental list of the ideas you carry around that seem like peace to you but when peeled off like a fruit's skin reveal a wrong belief about peace.

3. When we are at peace through resting in a relationship with God, we are kinder to others. Do you agree with this statement? Can you give an example of seeing this statement at work in your life or in the life of someone around you?

4. What do you think peace means to children? When they watch the news and see horrendous things happening, how can your new understanding of this fruit help them handle what they see?

Dear Jesus,

I have to admit that peace has always seemed to me to be the absence of hassle and hard things in life—and therefore beyond my control. Help me to apply the understanding that peace is the result of resting in a relationship with you in the midst of irritation, not just in the absence of it. When I'm bugged, help me to turn into your presence.

In your name, amen.

Peace I leave with you; my peace I give you. I do not give to you as the world gives. Do not let your hearts be troubled and do not be afraid.

John 14:27

eight

patience

hanging in there with hard-to-love people

A coconut is undoubtedly the toughest of all fruits. Its stonelike shell insulates from all but the most damaging of outer attacks and protects the sweet meat seed within.

Hurry up and wait. To most of us, patience is what we need when our schedules don't match up with life.

Usually we think of patience as perseverance through the most trying of circumstances. Racing to the doctor's office only to arrive and be told that he's running late.

Selecting the express lane at the market and then noticing the customer in front of us has overdone her limit of fourteen items. A weather delay ruining our return flight from a business trip. A traffic snarl keeping us from a preschool performance. There's a kind of patience that has to do with such aggravations: patience with situations.

But this isn't the kind of patience addressed in the Bible's fruit list. The word in the list actually means patience with people. It is patience with who people are, what they do that might bother or even offend us.

Oh.

This kind of patience is holding your hands back while your five-year-old creates her fifty-third-in-a-row set of bunny ears to loop (whoops; missed it again!) into a shoelace bow, all the while stubbornly puffing, "I can do it myself!" This kind of patience is sucking in our breath when our husband returns from the store with the wrong kind of cereal when we had specifically written down the name for him. This kind of patience is listening to a lonely friend who drones on and on and on about her life but shows little interest in ours.

I have a friend who let me down big-time. She'd promised to cover a commitment for me and then didn't. Her failure to follow through hurt others, and it hurt me. I looked carefully at my own responsibilities in the matter. Perhaps I shouldn't have delegated the job to her. Okay. But she'd *committed* to me. *She* messed up. *She* let me down. *She* blew it. I felt like blaming her and telling the whole world it was *her* fault, not mine.

Just about this time my son spilled a dose of orange decongestant on my cream-colored bathroom carpet. My first attempts at stain removal seemed to make it worse. The stain spread. But eventually, with enough water and rinsing and sopping, the orange lessened to peach and then to pink. Almost gone. And yet it still remained. This would take work, the chemical kind. After four applications of spot remover, the stain was finally out, or at least you couldn't see it through the suds of the cleaner.

Mistakes cause stains. And stains take work to remove. Similarly, someone has to *work* to remove the stain of sin. *Someone* did. Jesus has done the hardest part already. The work he did on the cross when he died to forgive all our errors is done. Now Jesus asks us to join his work. Our job is to receive his love and forgiveness and extend them to others.

Patience is hanging in there with hard-to-love people

> Patience is hanging in there with hard-to-love people . . . sometimes to the point of forgiveness but always to the point of love.

. . . sometimes to the point of forgiveness but always to the point of love. No wonder this fruit is so tough to peel, much less practice, in the raw day-to-day of life!

Admittedly, our natural response to people's offenses is hurt and anger and sometimes self-defense.

Patience doesn't mean slapping on a "nice" face and ignoring the reality of how we feel. When there's a bright orange stain in the middle of our cream-colored carpet, we can walk around it or cover it with a throw rug, but it's still there. Living as if it isn't won't do much for us or for those around us.

Emotions of pain and hurt in response to the offenses of others need to be processed and experienced because we are, by nature, emotional human beings. To deny such feelings is to deny who we are. But there is a way in which experiencing the hurt and anger and disappointment of offenses can lead to forgiveness. When we process our response to being wronged with God—honestly expressing to him how we feel—the fruit of patience can grow from the tangled vines of our hurt.

Patience doesn't mean slapping on a "nice" face and ignoring the reality of how we feel.

The naked truth about patience is that in order to have it, we must ask for it and cooperate with God in its growth in our relationships. Sure, all the fruits on the list grow only in relationship with the Gardener, who is God. We have to *want* him to grow them in us. We have to *allow* him to grow them in us. But patience seems to be one of the tough-to-grow fruits. When we get honest about it, we'd rather see love and peace popping up out of our soil than patience. Like me with my friend, blaming and grudge-bearing are so much more comfortable.

What does it look like to cooperate with God in the growth of patience? Sometimes patience might look like saying a prayer for the person who is bugging us. There are other moments when patience will direct us to lovingly confront the one who has offended. We might be pushed to love someone who's very hard to love because he or she has wounded us. There are still other occasions when we will find patience leading us to forgive a person for a bumbling blooper. And there are rare occasions when patience looks like creating space between us and people with problems because space is necessary for healing to occur.

Patience is hanging in there and staying with people who are hard to love at times. Friends. Husbands. Children, for sure. Parents. Bosses. Neighbors. Pastors. Coworkers.

Patience is more than a nice face put on in a not-so-nice moment when someone wounds us. It's a supernatural fruit. Patience is a spiritual fruit that grows from the soil of our humanity. As we experience unwelcome wounds from people, God can grow his fruit in our hearts and empower us to respond to such hurt with patience.

Fruit for Thought

1. Review the difference between patience with circumstances and patience with people. What skills are necessary to deal with both? What skills are uniquely important for dealing with hard-to-love people?
2. Time to get down to it. Are you holding on to a grudge, stuck in unforgiveness, or unable to move toward a person who has wounded you or someone

you love? Ask God to grow the fruit of patience in you for this specific relationship. Be honest about your emotions, as they need to be processed. Process what steps you might need to take to demonstrate patience in this spot in your life.

3. On the other hand, is there someone who needs patience with *you* because of a wound you've inflicted? What steps might you take to heal the matter from your end?

> *Dear Jesus,*
>
> *I'm thinking of _____. You know the situation. You were there. I feel _____ and _____ every time I remember this matter. Please help me release these emotions to you. They are real and I know it. Show me how patience would look in this situation. Help me to have the courage to demonstrate it, starting today.*
>
> *In your name, amen.*

Be patient, bearing with one another in love.

Ephesians 4:2

nine

kindness

meeting needs nicely

The pineapple has long stood as a symbol of hospitality. From Hawaii to New York, a pineapple as a present welcomes guests to a home and underlines their inclusion in a family's circle.

If there's one fruit that seems at first glance to fit the concept of "nice," it's kindness. To some of us kindness conveys a kind of syrupy-sweet offering of help for those less fortunate than we are. Let's be real. While kindness may well include extending care to those who have little in life, it does not demand a fake or formulaic offering of "niceness." And the needy are not the only folks in our lives who benefit from the fruit of kindness.

At its root, to be kind means to be "useful." Kindness is meeting needs.

Kindness is meeting needs.

Let's take apart this definition a bit. First, kindness is an action. Kindness notices that an elderly neighbor hasn't been out and about for a few days, so it knocks on her door and checks on her health. Kindness adopts an AIDS orphan in Africa and faithfully sends a support check each month. Kindness rinses a husband's dishes and picks up his socks just because he's running late and such gestures would help out. Kindness contains pure, clean action—the kind that usually costs us something in terms of time and energy.

Second, kindness is an action coupled with compassion. Kindness cares, and because it cares, it acts. Kindness gets involved. It picks up a pair of glasses someone dropped in a parking lot and turns them in at Lost and Found. It gives its seat on the bus to an elderly woman. It writes a check to a ministry to meet their needs because they've met the needs of so many. Kindness is action coupled with compassion.

At MOPS International, we hear stories of kindness—
offered mom to mom—that inspire our staff. Here's one:

I am a mom of seven children, ranging in age from eigh-
teen months to fifteen years. (A long-term career MOP!)
Last Christmas our family was going through an extremely
difficult financial situation. My MOPS group caught wind
of it and came to our side to help out. They all chipped in
and got each one of our children a gift. My husband and
I even received a gift. They also gave us food and treats,
and one personally gave us gift cards for groceries.

Things started to look up for us for a few months and
then we began to fall behind again financially. Once again,
my MOPS group was there for us. We received more gift
cards for groceries along with gifts.

One fellow mom did something a little differently. She
contacted a quilting group she belongs to. One by one,
patchwork pieces from different towns, states, and even
countries were sent to her. She put them all together
and created a beautiful quilt for me. She called it "a hug
for people who are going through difficult times." She
gave it to me with a matching pillow with this verse of
Scripture: "If one falls down, his friend can help him up.

But pity the man who falls and has no none to help him up!" (Eccles. 4:10).

Kindness is meeting needs; it's action coupled with compassion.

It's one thing to muster up such a response for the once-a-year clothing drive for the homeless, or provide school supplies for inner-city kids, or take a meal to a mom. But you know where kindness is the most costly? At home.

Oh.

> **Kindness is meeting needs; it's action coupled with compassion.**

It's hard to express kindness to those we know well, and even more challenging to be constantly kind to those we know best. Behind the closed curtains of home, our charitable smiles fade, and our willingness to help out winds down with the wearying messes and needs and questions. We snarl at the guy we loved enough to marry. We turn churlish toward our cherished children. In the middle of a tirade about how no one ever takes their shoes or books or toys up the stairs, the phone rings and we automatically adjust our tone from Malcolm in the Middle Mother Shrill to a polished and professional Oprah, "Hello?"

We try. Truly, we do. But to tell the truth, we seem to do a better job extending kindness outside our homes than inside.

I wonder why.

Of course we're tired. More tired inside home than outside. And the needs there are never-ending. They don't stop at 5:00 or 8:00 or even 11:00. We can control the influences and interruptions coming from outside our home, or at least choose which ones we'll respond to. Inside . . . well, meeting needs is what we're there for, isn't it? We can't let the phone ring or not answer the door when it comes to family. When a child is sick, who else but Mom will fetch a cold washcloth? When a husband hits a schedule bump, of course we'll be the one to pinch-hit for him!

A major truth for moms or any caretaker is that we can't give to others what we don't have ourselves. Oh, we think we're being incredibly selfless and spiritually mature to give to others while ignoring our own needs. But are we?

Get naked now! Peel it! Even Jesus didn't ignore his

own needs 24/7. Kindness to others begins with kindness to ourselves. Think of it this way. What if it's *less* kind to ignore ourselves so that we're run-down grouches and *more* kind to do enough self-care to change our attitude? What if that's what Jesus meant when he encouraged us all to love our neighbor as we love ourselves? What if receiving God's love and kindness toward ourselves is what it means to look like Jesus in this attribute of kindness? See, we can be kind to others only when we continue to replenish our tank of kindness by being kind to ourselves.

Let's bring this fruit home—literally. In order to be kind to our family, we need to be kind to "me."

The naked fruit of kindness is meeting needs. Kindness is acting to meet needs with compassion. Rather than some archaic manner of chivalry or a syrupy-sweet "niceness," kindness is getting up and meeting a need because it's there and we care.

Fruit for Thought

1. Do you try to give what you don't have? Go to the King of Kindness. When we're running on empty in our kindness tank, it helps to remember how kind

God has been to us. Name five specific actions God has taken to demonstrate his kindness in your life.

2. Are you kind to yourself? After focusing on receiving God's kindness, practice kindness toward yourself. Make room in your day or night for an activity that meets *your* need. A bath. A cup of tea. A chapter in a book. Five minutes of quiet. It doesn't have to be a huge deal, but when you treat yourself with an act of kindness, you'll be better able to do the same with others. What practice of kindness can you begin for *you*?

3. Determine to wake up with kindness. Turn around the myth that kindness is best expressed outside the home. Instead, start your kindness at home. Be intentional about being kind to those you love the most and watch how your actions and attitude multiply to those outside your walls. Which family member could use your kindness right now? What action could you take to demonstrate kindness today?

Dear Jesus,

I have to admit, I'm running on empty when it comes to kindness at home! There doesn't seem to be enough of me. But I know there is always enough of you. Please show me how to receive the kindness you have for me, to be kind to myself, and then out of that fullness, to share kindness with those I love the most.

In your name, amen.

Be kind and compassionate to one another.

Ephesians 4:32

ten

goodness

being like God inside and out

The strawberry wears its seeds on the outside. With no apologies, this tangy fruit proclaims its nature, sharing its seeds as it grows.

We use the word *good* loosely. We apply it to dogs, days, parties, to anything we measure. But in a spiritual sense, what is goodness?

As a fruit of the Spirit, the word *good* means what is excellent in character or constitution. It is to be morally sound. Goodness is . . . well . . . perfection.

Great. How are we ever going to get that fruit growing in our lives?

Since spiritual fruits are characteristics of God exhibited in our unique personalities, we can begin by understanding the goodness of God. There's a verse in the Bible that offers some clarity on God's goodness. Referring to God, the psalmist writes, "You are good, and what you do is good" (Psalm 119:68). It's simple and I like that.

God is good in his being. His character is good. Ask any mom what she's teaching her child, and on the list will be something such as "to be good." It's not natural to us. We have to try to be good. But goodness is totally natural to God.

God is also good in his actions. God does good things. His actions are always consistent with his character. When the Bible says that God is good, it means he acts in good ways in our lives for his good purpose. And just what is that purpose? To make us good.

Maybe you remember a little prayer you said when you were a child: "God is great. God is good. Let us thank him for our food." We know God is great. We believe he is good. But we stub our toe on doubts when the next logical question forms. Is God good to me?

100

Sometimes we know that God is good to us. Our precious children fill our hearts with gladness. Money stretches to meet all our needs with a little extra for a meal out, a new outfit, and even that sofa we've been eyeing. God is good to give us what we need to be happy. When our lives are full and we have what we want, we enjoy his goodness. In such moments we think, *God is great. God is good. And . . . yep, he's good to me.*

Other times, we wonder, *Is he really good—to me?* Our child becomes ill, very ill. We lose our income. There's not enough money for extras and barely enough for food and clothes. Life is challenging. Our parents cease to be able to care for themselves. Fun goes down the drain, and in its place, suffering bubbles to the surface. God doesn't seem good to us anymore.

What's happened? Between the "God is good to me" moments and the "Is he really good to me?" times, what changes? It isn't God. The Bible teaches he is the same yesterday, today, and tomorrow. God doesn't change. He's either good when good *and* bad things happen, or he's not good when either happens. What changes is our view of God. When times are good, we see his goodness. When times are tough—well—it can be hard to see his goodness.

Perhaps it helps to tease apart the difference between kindness and goodness. At its root, kindness has to do with what we do. Goodness concerns who we are. Kindness, as we covered in the last chapter, is a useful fruit that has as its goal meeting needs. Goodness, on the other hand, sees the needs but doesn't necessarily purpose to meet them. Why? Because the goal of goodness is to make us like God. And God's meeting our needs doesn't always accomplish such an objective.

> Kindness has to do with what we do. Goodness concerns who we are.

Just as God is good to give us what makes us happy, he is happy to give us what makes us good. His actions consistently push us to the point where we will eventually resemble him. Sometimes that means withholding what we think we want in order to provide what he knows we need. He knows that we seem to grow more during the lean times than during the full times of life.

Wait. Am I saying that God makes horrible stuff happen to us so that we'll be more like him? No. That's not what the Bible teaches. But God can and does use the hardest of times to help us grow. He won't waste them. He is as present in the unhappy, unfulfilled moments as he is in the happy times.

How does a good God grow such a good fruit in our lives? He begins the seed of this fruit on our insides—in our beings—and grows it outward to our actions. Goodness is becoming like God, inside and out, in our beings and in our actions, through good and bad times.

I remember learning this inside-out kind of lesson about goodness when my son, Ethan, was ten or eleven. He came stomping in from play, steamed because his friend had excluded him from a game of street hockey. While I wanted to call the friend's mom and insist that her son include my little darling in his precious game, I held back and instead worked with Ethan on his temper.

> Goodness is becoming like God, inside and out, in our beings and in our actions, through good and bad times.

But the next morning, Ethan came to breakfast, still in a rotten mood. He grunted at me, refused to respond to my questions, and rolled his eyes at my commands that he rearrange his attitude. Hey, I'd fixed him, hadn't

I? What was wrong with him? Why didn't he move past this spot? Now I was steamed.

Breakfast dishes were spread across the counter. Grabbing juice glasses and coffee cups, I shoved them in their wire partitions in the top rack of the dishwasher. The clock showed five minutes to the first school bell. And we were still here, in a mess. My anger grew. I threw the dishwasher door up, clanging it against the still-extended upper rack and shoving rack, glasses, and cups back into their hole in one singular motion. The catch caught with a click, and I heard a slight tinkling sound from within.

Yikes. Carefully, I opened the dishwasher door. More tinkling sounds. Tentatively, I peered inside. Shards from what used to be three juice glasses hung at odd angles from the upper rack. I lifted one coffee cup, chipped but still intact, and a concept taught in the Bible filtered through my thinking. I remembered Jesus telling the teachers of the law that they were hypocritical because they worried about the outside of their lives looking good but never addressed the deeper issues of greed and selfishness within. He said, "First clean the inside of the cup and dish, and then the outside also will be clean" (Matt. 23:26).

Whoops. That's what I was doing with Ethan. Fixing

his display of temper on the outside—making it all look good—and forgetting about the inside.

But that's not what matters to God. God cares about us being good the way he is good. So he gives us good opportunities for this fruit to grow. Goodness works from the inside out. It starts with who we are in our beings. Left to ourselves, we're like those teachers in the Bible who only worried about outward appearance. They weren't so good on the inside. But when God comes in and does a little housecleaning in our hearts, forgiving our errors and making us clean internally, then we're good inside out, in our beings as well as in our actions. Goodness can't be clothed in superficiality and still be good. At its core, goodness is nakedly good.

> Goodness works from the inside out.

God is good in his being and in his actions, in who he is and in what he does. The fruits of the Spirit are his characteristics evidenced in our personalities. We can't be good on the outside without God first making us good on the inside. Once this process begins, it grows goodness in us, from the inside out. Through good times and bad, the fruit of goodness grows us to be like God, inside and out.

Fruit for Thought

1. What's the difference between inside and outside goodness? Think of this example: We might compliment a friend on her cooking, saying she's a good cook (action) without meaning she's a good woman (being). How does this inside/out distinction apply to you with your family, children, husband, neighbors, co-workers? Are you good on the inside and not on the out, or vice versa?

2. C. S. Lewis believed that goodness isn't kindness, because kindness simply wants to offer compassion in the face of suffering and doesn't care whether something is changed in the long run. Process the difference between kindness and goodness a bit. What is the goal of kindness? What is the goal of goodness? Why are both named as fruits of the Spirit?

3. Why do you think that goodness is so important to God? Can you identify some spots where you resist God's fruit of goodness and why?

4. If goodness begins on the inside, it makes sense that we start there in cooperating with God to grow this

fruit in our lives. Where in your inner thoughts and attitudes do you wish you were more like Jesus?

Dear Jesus,

I have to admit that I'm not sure I like goodness that much: being made like you inside and out. It seems so hard. But in the long run, goodness will help me grow. I know that. Please start with my inside to make me good. Clean me up and make me new. Then, I pray, grow this inner goodness into my outer actions. I also pray that I will grow more and more in my desire for you to make both me and those around me good. I realize that might involve enduring some struggles that don't look good to me. But I trust you to be good in your being and your actions, and I agree with your purpose to make us good.

In your name, amen.

And we know that in all things God works for the good of those who love him.

Romans 8:28

eleven

faithfulness

being true to God

---

*No fruit is more "everyday" than the apple. You can count on
an apple. Its easily identifiable form—red or green or gold skin,
white pulp, and black seeds—labels it as the "essential" fruit for
life. An apple a day . . . !*

One late afternoon as I completed a walk through my
neighborhood, I had an experience that would forever
shape my life. As I approached my house, I noticed a
side gate—one I'd never before seen. How could that be?
Surprised, I checked my bearings—was this indeed my
house? It was, and I made my way to the gate.

With my hand on the latch, I examined the gate, seemingly not there when I left, now present. It was a simple but elegant gate, made of wood with iron hardware. It swung open easily and silently at my touch.

Before me was a brick path leading through a beautiful tangle of flowers, but what caught my eye and held my gaze was the stand of trees in the distance: an orchard of fruit-bearing beauties that stretched eternally into the distance.

I glanced over my shoulder to see if a neighbor—anyone—was there to take in this impossible sight, but no, I remained alone. Cautiously and yet unable to resist, I stepped onto the path and shut the gate behind me.

While the flowers were fragrant and lovely, the trees drew me, and I found myself standing beneath them, head upturned as I gazed at their heavy-laden branches. Such fruit I'd never seen! What lush, vivid produce! The branches dipped with the weight. The fruit dewed with readiness, begging me to bite.

Just then, I noticed I wasn't alone after all. A gardener made his way toward me from a corner of the orchard, offering a casual smile as he approached. In his hands were several gardening tools. The pockets of his overalls contained seed packets and other essentials for his work. He reached me and offered a worn but firm hand as a welcome. Though still in my own backyard, I sensed I was somehow on his turf.

He spoke. "How do you like your orchard?"

"My orchard?" I responded.

"Yes. I planted it for you right in your backyard that you might walk in it with me every day and every night. It's yours. A gift from me."

I gazed in amazement at the pure lavishness of the landscape. "But how can this be? My backyard is nothing like this! It's tiny! And unkempt! And everything I try to grow dies because of the poor soil, the hot sun, and the lack of water. I'll never be able to keep such an orchard healthy!"

The gardener surveyed the orchard and then turned his eyes back to me. "You don't have to worry about any of that. I have planted this orchard in your life for you. I will care for it. I will keep it healthy. I will be faithful to fulfill what I have planted here.

"I only ask a few things of you in response. I will be here every day, working on this orchard. I want you to come and be with me each day. I will wait for you. I want to walk with you here so that I can explain the ways of the orchard to you. At times my work in your orchard will not be pleasant to you. I will prune branches that are not growing. I will stake up those that are leaning in the wrong direction. I will transplant trees that need a better location. I may even remove growth as it becomes sickly or dies. As I do my work, I want you to remember that my goal is that your orchard grows as fully and as freely as possible so that you and others in your life can fully enjoy its fruit.

"Do you want this orchard in your life?" he asked as he looked directly into my eyes.

"Oh yes!" How could I not?

"Will you meet me here each day on the bench under the apple tree?" He gestured with his hand.

"Of course!" I responded.

He nodded in pleased agreement while I hurried to the bench at that moment and sat down with the gardener and opened my heart.

The next morning I awoke to my normal routine of breakfast-making, kitchen-tidying and children-preparing so as to get out for my day. I remembered the orchard. I went to the window, opened the blinds, and stood, taking it in. Indeed, it was as real as the day before: beautiful and lush in its fruit. I determined to return to my house early in the afternoon for a time with the gardener.

That first day I was able to adjust my schedule to return early. I settled the children at play and made my way out through the gate. Sure enough, just as he had promised, the gardener waited for me on the bench. What a delight that conversation with him turned out to be! The time flew, and I discovered a latent interest in the subjects he described that I'd never imagined within me! As the sunlight faded, I hurried back to my children, already eager for the next day and more time with the gardener.

The next day I arrived only a few minutes late, and instead of finding the gardener on the bench, I noticed him down one row of trees on a ladder, sawing off branches in such a way that the tree looked lopsided, uneven, ugly. I didn't like what I saw. Where the tree had covered the sight, now a view of the industrial side of the city could be seen. Warehouses stood pressed against each other. Smokestacks spit out steel-colored smoke. I didn't like this view. I preferred the fruit-filled branches of my tree in my orchard.

When the gardener sensed my irritation, he turned to

me and said, "Remember, I warned you that you might not care for all of my maneuvers in the orchard. You must trust me that I am able to care for the orchard better than you and allow me room to work here."

I sighed and agreed, but our time together was tense, and I found my heart withdrawing a bit.

The next day one child was sick, so I sat at the window and looked out at the orchard. I could see the gardener waiting on the bench, but I didn't feel free to go to him. Why I didn't open the window and call out to him, I don't know. But that day went by without a visit to the orchard.

The next day passed and somehow I grew busy and didn't even look out the window. There was laundry to fold, a project to complete, an errand to run. The blinds were shut from the evening before; I didn't take the time to open them.

Weeks passed. The rains came. Then snow. And then spring.

One morning I opened the blinds almost unconsciously as had become my habit and went about my morning routine. With the changing of the season, the sun filtered through the blinds at a new angle and pierced my sight as I sipped my coffee and read the newspaper. I looked up.

Oh, the orchard! And the gardener! How could I have forgotten the miraculous work going on in my own backyard? I hurried for a sweater and threw open the gate. There, in the distance, was the bench. And there, sitting comfortably, was the gardener, waiting for me.

"Have you been here all this time?" I asked incredulously.

"I told you I would be," he replied.

I looked about me at the orchard in bloom, fruit on its way. "And the orchard, is it still growing?"

"Yes, as I promised, it is still growing. I took on the responsibility of growing it, and I will not stop."

My heart ached as I realized that this gardener had been faithful to plant, to stake, to water, and to prune, just as he had promised, and yet I had not been faithful to come to see him as I had promised. As I thought back over my life for those past months, I realized that I'd had very little growth in my days outside the orchard. I had become impatient, irritable, and even greedy in some of my relationships. The gardener had been faithfully growing my orchard in my own backyard, but I'd been living as if it didn't exist.

My imaginary orchard has taught me many truths about life, specifically about faithfulness. The spiritual fruit of faithfulness is an active response to God's faithfulness. As he keeps his promises to us, we mirror his faithfulness by keeping ours to him. Faithfulness is being true to God. It's keeping our commitment to him in the way he keeps his commitment to us.

We mirror God's faithfulness by being true to him and true to others.

True to God? God wants to spend time with us, so we spend time with him by reading the Bible, by praying, and by being a part of a faith community in a church.

True to others? God wants us to be like Jesus in our relationships with others. That means being dependable, loyal, committed, and true to others with integrity and follow-through. This second dimension of faithfulness is the arena where we can act out the faithfulness that grows in our times with God.

> We mirror God's faithfulness by being true to him and true to others.

The naked truth about faithfulness is that it just may be the hardest of all fruits to grow in our lives. Not because it's hard for God. He's there, waiting. It's tough for us to go to him to receive what he wants to give us. There's nothing nice about our withdrawal. We forget. We may not believe he's really there. We think other things are more important. And so we are faithless to God and offer a faithless effort of investment to those around us.

> Faithfulness may be the hardest of all fruits to grow in our lives.

But when we just go to him—just go—his faithfulness is enough to provide faithfulness in us. Faithfulness is being true to God, and as we are true to God, we can be true to others.

Fruit for Thought

1. Have you ever experienced unfaithfulness in a relationship in which someone was not true to you? Describe the emotions you faced. How have you recovered from that experience? What lessons have you brought forward in life as a result?

2. Name someone who has been faithful to you. What did such faithfulness feel like? How did such faithfulness affect your life? How does such faithfulness motivate you to respond?

3. Now consider a relationship in which you are being asked to be faithful. How successful are you? What is the easiest part of faithfulness to this person? What is the most challenging? How can you improve your faithfulness?

4. Is it possible to be 100 percent faithful to God and to others? Why or why not? How does your answer shape your efforts with this fruit?

> *Dear Jesus,*
>
> *I am in awe of your faithfulness to me. To think that you are constantly available to me is beyond my comprehension. I don't think I've ever had such an offer in a human relationship. And yet there are so many times when I overlook your faithfulness and ignore your offer to be in a relationship. I'm sorry. Please help me to choose to be with you more often so that I am acting out my desire to be true to you. And please help me to act out your faithfulness to me by being faithful to others you*

put in my life: my children, my parents, my husband, and my friends. May I mirror your faithfulness in the lives of those around me.

In your name, amen.

If we are faithless, he will remain faithful.

2 Timothy 2:13

twelve

gentleness

yielding ourselves to God

The banana is a sensitive fruit. Its skin provides incomplete protection. Often if its skin is bruised, so is the fruit within.

We live in a world where those who wrestle their way to the top are esteemed. Gentleness is wimpiness. Nobody wants to waste time being gentle when success is spelled T-O-U-G-H.

Many Bible authorities hold that the word for gentleness in the fruit list is the most difficult of all to translate into our language and culture. Centuries ago the philosopher Aristotle described this word as "the golden mean between extreme anger and extreme angerlessness."

I like best a usage of the word that predates even Aristotle. A young soldier fighting in the Peloponnesian wars wrote to his sweetheart about a gift he was bringing her: a white stallion. "He is the most magnificent animal I've ever seen, but he responds obediently to the slightest command. . . . He allows his master to direct him to his full potential. He is truly a meek [gentle] horse."

> Gentleness is harnessed power; it is a bent will.

When we look at the historical background of the word for gentleness, we get a picture of gentleness that is anything but weak. Gentleness is harnessed power; it is a bent will. Taken from the picture of a wild animal tamed to reach its potential, gentleness is a soul yielded to God's desires.

Whoa. Now you're talking T-O-U-G-H.

There are many mothering moments in which to practice growing this fruit. I remember one in particular. It took place one summer, during the neighborhood prelims for the swim team championships. My daughter, Eva, was a

122

swimmer—an amazing talent in my humble estimation. The top eight finishers from two heats would make it to finals. I was feeling confident.

I stood on the side, timer poised for the gun. Her dive was good. Straight off the block. Not too deep. She surfaced smoothly and began stroking. Quick, even strokes, slapping through the water. She came to the turn. A little slow . . . then she picked up speed again. Just a few more meters. She touched. Second in her heat. Good. After the next heat, I surmised she'd be third overall.

The finalists were posted. A mom came to tell me, "Eva made it!"

"Great!" I cheered. "What place was she?"

"Sixth," came her reply.

And then out of my mouth came the words, "Only sixth? You're kidding! What happened?"

I looked down at Eva. There she sat beside me, water dripping down her neck from under her cap, the flush of exertion still in her cheeks. My words echoed back to me. What more did I want? What was wrong with sixth? After all, places didn't matter in prelims. It was only necessary to make the top eight to qualify. And besides that, she was only nine years old in a neighborhood championship for nine-year-olds. What did I want?

I leaned down and whispered, "I just blew it, didn't I?" Eva nodded. I teared up and swallowed. "I'm sorry," I offered. She shrugged.

I've thought a lot about my response that day. Through the championships and in the years since, I've wondered about my gut reaction. What *did* I want? Did I want my daughter to be a champion so she would have friends and acclaim? Did I want her to win so I'd be applauded? Did I want her to beat the whole lot just because it would be fun and she could do it?

Probably all of the above. But one day in the distant future, what difference would it make?

I think back to my poolside behavior and all the arrow prayers I had flung heavenward. Sure, I believed God cared about the details of my days and welcomed any and all of my concerns. But there I was, dragging my agenda around the lawn chairs, insisting on the fulfillment of my concept of good for Eva.

It's a small example, but it represents a lifetime of growing the fruit of gentleness. Being yielded to God's desires means letting go of mine.

Mothers, beware. Gentleness is a tricky fruit to grow because it requires such surrender, and surrender makes us vulnerable. Oh baby, so very vulnerable. When we admit that we don't really get to pick and choose what will happen or not happen to our children or who they will or won't become, we recognize that what we're investing in their young days has an ending point. Eventually they will gather up the heap of stuff we've offered over the years, throw it in the trunks of their cars, and head off on their own. They might purpose to grow a life that matters—themselves—or they might not. And we don't get to choose. They do.

> Being yielded to God's desires means letting go of mine.

I just have to admit, I don't like this part of mothering. To be honest (naked!), I don't like this part of life. As hard as it is to relinquish control over my kids and how they'll turn out in life, it's equally hard to let go of command-central of my own days. You mean God knows what's better for me and for who I want to become than I do? No way!

Yes way.

Gentleness is the fruit of the Spirit that yields. Giant yellow triangular sign obeyed, gentleness pauses, looks both ways, and waits for directions before proceeding. With kids. With work. With friendships. With a mate. With parents. And with what we do to become who we want to be.

Fruit for Thought

1. The definition of gentleness given in this chapter probably sounds nothing like what you thought gentleness would be. What preconceptions did you have about this fruit? How did those preconceptions shape your surface like or dislike of this fruit? Admit it: Were you really looking forward to this one?

2. In what areas of your life have you seen God growing the fruit of gentleness, helping you to yield your desires to his? Now . . . tougher question: Where are you still wrestling for control?

3. Like a banana that easily bruises, we do become more vulnerable as the fruit of gentleness grows in our lives. What precautions do we need to take as we allow God to grow this fruit? Is there such a thing as being too gentle, too yielded, or yielded to the wrong thing?

Dear Jesus,

You alone are my safety zone. I yield to you. Cover me with your love and protection as I yield my choices to your desires. Help me especially with my children. Oh, how much I want them to love you and your ways and to live lives that matter! But, God, I put them into your hands to accomplish that desire. I recognize that I don't get to choose who they become, but I do get to choose Whom I will turn to with my desires for them.

In your name, amen.

But we were gentle among you, like a mother caring for her little children.

1 Thessalonians 2:7

thirteen

self-control

being healthy-minded

The orange is perhaps the fruit that most symbolizes health. Its vitamin C is prescribed for treatment of everything from the common cold to a wrinkled complexion.

It had been a loooooooonnnnng day. It was late. I felt like one of those cardboard juice boxes—except there had been about fourteen straws stuck in me, and everybody around me had been taking a draw all day. I was sucked dry.

Then came the requests for a shirt to be washed in an extra, special load; for mac and cheese instead of hamburgers; and—ooops!—for a dozen cookies for the bake sale that no one had informed me was the next day.

I tried to hold it together. I took a deep breath. I thought about my "happy place." But somehow, the Monster Mom inside me snuck through a tiny hole in the wall around my emotions and made a break for it. She was out!

"Is the mother the only person in this family who can wash a shirt?" she bellowed. Monster Mom wheeled toward the laundry room, snatching the soiled shirt in her grip, and plunged it into the washing machine.

"Is the mother the only person in this family who can make mac and cheese?" she screeched. Monster Mom slammed a saucepan into the sink, filling it to overflowing with hot water to boil. (Who was it that was boiling here?)

"Is the mother the only person in this family who can keep track of what needs to be done and when?" she escalated as she smacked a cookie sheet on the counter, attacking it with store-bought dough.

Yep, Monster Mom was on the loose all right. Oh, I try to keep her penned up inside. There is a thick, tall, imposing, and supposed-to-be impenetrable wall around my inner being that keeps her in her place, unable to damage others or me. But sometimes she scrapes open a spot and escapes. I've discovered she's very resourceful. She can get through the tiniest of gaps.

Is there a hole in your wall? Is there a spot where you tend to give way over and over again? Is it in the area of impatience? Imperfection? Temptation? Is there a tiny gap, barely noticeable, or a gaping gash, through which all your good intentions hurry out?

There's a proverb that says, "Like a city whose walls are broken down is a [person] who lacks self-control" (Prov. 25:28). In ancient days, the wall of the city protected it against invasion from enemies. Even a small opening in a wall meant that the entire city lay open to attack. Self-control hems us about, protecting us from losing ground to impatience, bitterness, greed, and the like.

> Self-control hems us about, protecting us from losing ground to impatience, bitterness, greed, and the like.

Most literally, the word *self-control* comes from two roots: one meaning to rein in or curb and the other meaning to heal, save, or make whole. These roots apply particularly to our sensitive nature, our understanding, and our mind. Thus, to be self-controlled is to be "healthy-minded." Self-control is a healthy-mindedness that watches for the holes in the walls of our lives and keeps them patched.

We're late getting the kids to bed because we couldn't tear ourselves away from the latest reality show finale. We're twenty pounds overweight, and although our clothes are too tight and we're way uncomfortable, we down another bag of chips and salsa. The credit card balance creeps up and up, but we go ahead and buy one more pair of shoes at the mall. We planned to get up a half hour early to spend a few minutes alone with God. But when the alarm goes off, we punch snooze until there's no choice but to skip God and hurry out the door.

Like the first in a row of dominoes giving way, a hole appears in the wall around our lives and grows larger with each temptation until it gives way to a gap large enough for Monster Mom, Shopaholic, Fat Mama, and the like to burst through. Pretty soon we're too weary to fight. Whatever. The hole's just too big now. Let it rip!

It's never too late to repair the wall. It may seem so. In fact, that's one of the greatest lies in our days: It's too late, it's too big, it's too bad, forget it. But because the fruit of self-control, like all spiritual fruit, is a fruit grown by God in our lives, it's not too late today and it won't be too late tomorrow. That's what's so great about God! He doesn't give up on us, so we don't have to give up on ourselves!

Now. What to do when there's a hole in your wall?

First, go back to the definition of self-control: healthy-mindedness. The holes in our walls are patched when we learn to think truthfully about our lives in a healthy-minded fashion. What's the truth about who I am and what I do and what I want to be? A life that matters is a life connected to God. If I'm connected, I'm growing in the fruit of the Spirit—love, joy, peace, patience, kindness, goodness, faithfulness, gentleness, and self-control—and that reality will grow in me and through me a life that matters.

> A life that matters is a life connected to God.

Then apply this healthy-minded thinking to all the areas of life: your body, your relationships, and your importance in life. Most of us unwittingly believe lies about who we are and what we're worth. Fueled by our upbringings, fed by the media's warped views, we swallow falsehoods and base our choices on myths. Self-control is a healthy-minded manner of thinking that helps us undo such crazy thinking.

What's the truth about your body? Is a model-perfect body the only "right" kind of body? On the other hand, is it healthy to just let our body blob out? What's the truth about your mind? Are you feeding it a diet of soap-opera mythology? It's hard to be happy with reality when we're constantly gazing at fantasy. How about your expectations of yourself as a mom? When we constantly compare ourselves to others, we find we're never good enough.

You get the drift.

It's amazing how unhealthy thinking affects us. Like a prisoner sawing through the defenses built to protect us and keep us sane, unhealthy thinking begins in our minds and then escapes to affect our overall satisfaction with life.

Think healthy-mindedly. Apply healthy thinking to all the areas of your life. And keep it practical.

Start small. Pick one hole at a time for patching. Junk food. TV. Perfectionism. Don't try to tackle every spot at once. You'll do better when you build a series of small victories.

Keep disciplined company. It's so much easier to jog at 6:30 in the morning if you have a friend meeting you at the corner. Hang out with others who are healthy-minded and find strength in each other's company.

Work first and then play. If you try this the other way around, chances are you won't make much forward progress. You may even slide backward.

Reward yourself. Self-control doesn't mean depriving yourself. Enjoy the good stuff when you reach a goal. A bag of peanut M&M's after reaching a weight-loss goal, a girls' night out after completing a project on time. Good stuff has a good place in a healthy life.

It's easy—tempting!—to misuse self-control by either overdoing control (that can become obsession) or even applying self-control to spots in life that are meant to be out of our control (like taking responsibility for all of our children's actions!). Peel off the extras of self-control and get naked about self-control by allowing it to be the fruit

God means it to be and no more. Part of healthy-mindedness includes the creation of healthy boundaries by which we opt for control over our own issues and relinquish efforts toward issues that belong to others.

Self-control is healthy-mindedness. This is the fruit that patches the holes in the walls of our lives, protecting us from our worst temptations and desires. "Is the mother the only one in the family who can fix the hole in her wall?"

Want the naked truth? It's not nice, but, yep, 'fraid so.

Fruit for Thought

1. Look around you. The commercials on TV. The displays in stores. The checkout line at the market. What messages about self-control do you encounter in your daily activities? How do these messages either shore up or break down your wall?
2. Take a walk around the wall of your life and look for existing openings as well as spots that show signs of giving way. List them for yourself. Temptations. Emotions. Relationships. Attitudes. Addictions. Can you prioritize those that are most important for your immediate attention? What spots can wait? Before

you set these spots aside, consider what damage might be done by a complete lack of attention. Now finish your prioritization and then start patching through healthy-mindedness. Check back over the steps in the chapter as you get started.

3. Is there such a thing as too much control? Why or why not? In what area of your life might this become an issue for you? How can the growth of another fruit, such as joy or peace, help you to relinquish over-control in this area of your life?

4. How is the fruit of self-control growing in the lives of your children? How can you assist its growth? While we all want to see our children happy, when we model for them the discipline of self-control by delaying gratification, by saying no, by allowing them to experience the consequences of their actions rather than rescuing them, self-control grows in their days. Take a few minutes to think this through in your mothering.

Dear Jesus,

Thank you for showing me where holes are growing in the wall around my life. I know I can't patch all these holes without your help. Please show me where I have believed lies about myself, my past, and my present, and help me to replace these lies with the truth.

In your name, amen.

Be transformed by the renewing of your mind.

Romans 12:2

part three

fruit-filled living

>> getting honest about growing a life that matters

fourteen

fruit inspectors

how can we evaluate our fruit?

How's the produce section of your life? Are your orchards yielding a good crop of God's fruit? Living a life that matters means inspecting and evaluating our fruit. Take a craisin, for instance.

A craisin is a dried cranberry. Actually, it's not even that. A craisin is really the dried *remains* of a cranberry after all the juice has been extracted—the outer shell after the inner meat has been discarded. It carries few nutrients, but it's a good source of fiber. Some entrepreneurial farmer interested in utilizing all parts of the cranberry came up with the concept of sprinkling these little numbers on salads and in pilafs for color and texture.

Are there any craisins in your life? There are in mine. I've had my share of craisin days. Some mornings I'm growling at my husband in the bathroom before either of us has even entered the shower to wash away sleepiness. Sometimes a gritchy mood while carpooling sends me into a tirade about homework. And I remember one interchange at a UPS mailing center when, after hauling in box after box at Christmastime and receiving a craisin-like response from the counter worker, I retaliated with my own dried-up attitude. As I exited, she remarked that I'd been a speaker at her church's retreat earlier that year. Great.

Craisin days have a way of creating craisin lives. Dried up. Few nutrients. Good for little but fiber to flush away waste.

Are you living a fruit-filled life? Are your orchards yielding a good crop of God's fruit?

Love. Joy. Peace. Patience. Kindness. Goodness. Faithfulness. Gentleness. Self-control. The fruits of the Spirit are those characteristics that God produces in our lives when we're connected to him. Their exact expression will vary a bit from personality to personality, but basically the fruits of the Spirit are those qualities we possess when we look like Jesus. Fruit makes us better than we would be otherwise. It empowers us to extend ourselves to others in ways that make a difference. Spiritual fruit markets God's nature to the world around us. The Gardener responsible for growing these fruits in our lives is God, although we must cooperate with him in the growing process. Growing the fruit of the Spirit in our lives results in a life that matters, in us and in all that we invest in our world.

So how's it going, or should I say, growing? What kind of stuff is being produced in your life? Is the bulk of your crop made up of pouch-packaged craisins, or are there other fruits on display in the produce section of your life?

Not sure? Here's how you can check. Two qualities measure spiritual fruit: quality and quantity. Let's take them one at a time.

> Two qualities measure spiritual fruit: quality and quantity.

Quality. Are you growing genuine fruit that authentically represents God? Or have a few plastic pieces found their way into the fruit bin?

Beyond the distortion of dried cranberries, plastic fruit offers an even emptier promise. Plastic fruit looks like real fruit. Often it even feels like real fruit—or better! But under the pressure of adversity, it melts. Plastic fruit offers a feast for the eye while starving the stomach.

Oh, but it's so popular! Indeed. In place of love, we choose lust. Joy is replaced by temporary happiness. Peace trades places with contentment. Patience never buds when a fake, smiley niceness takes over and cuts off hard relationships. Kindness mutates into manipulation. Goodness is good-enough-ness. Faithfulness is a suck-it-up steadiness of our own making. Gentleness turns wimpy and yields to "whatever." Self-control is ritualistic compulsivity.

Bite into that. (And then spit it back out.)

You know what it's like, this plastic variety. Fake! "Sure I can find time to take your kids; I love spending time with them!" (When you can't and you don't.) Or "Oh, honey, I'd love to help you out, but I'm sooo busy with the kids right now!" (When you wouldn't and you're not.) One woman I know called this kind of plastic response "beauty-pageanting it." (For those readers who have actually participated in beauty pageants, this refers only to the most *stereotypical* of pageant moments.) When confronted with bumpy spots in life, she smiles sweetly, looks just left over someone's head, and basically invents some sweet-sounding response even if it isn't true. She thinks it's nicer than telling the truth, and in her mind it's more spiritual. Well, maybe it is nicer, but it's not more like Jesus.

Plastic fruit is not the real thing. And it can't substitute for the genuine offering of true spiritual fruit. Naked fruit is the real thing. It can't be counterfeited. There's no way to fake it. Pinch gentleness and its skin will bruise. Hack open patience and you'll find it sticking with you. With naked goodness, what you see is what you get. And self-control experienced in one arena brings the benefit of healthy-mindedness to every area of life.

Naked fruit is real fruit. We don't have to dress it up to make it better. Naked fruit can be honest. It can say, "Oh, I'd like to help, but I'm so exhausted!" or "Honey, I'm busy this morning; could I help you this afternoon when the baby is napping?" Naked fruit is not *always* available, or happy, or in a good mood. But naked fruit does rise up from the roots of dependency on God and tries, honestly, purely, and openly.

Beware of plastic fruit that offers the benefit of the real thing but delivers nothing; naked fruit is the real thing.

Beware of plastic fruit that offers the benefit of the real thing but delivers nothing; naked fruit is the real thing.

Check out the quality of your life's produce section.

Next? *Quantity.* The fruit of the Spirit is intended as a cluster. Love. Joy. Peace. Patience. Kindness. Goodness. Faithfulness. Gentleness. Self-control. They grow in bunches. Together. If you find a picked-apart cluster, a vine adorned with a few measly fruit, you may have settled for selective fruit growing. Love. Gentleness. Self-control. No joy anywhere to be found. In the spot where peace should be displayed, nothing.

God intended his fruit to grow in clusters of characteristics—all nine at once. When he's growing an example of what he looks like, he strives to illustrate all the aspects of his nature, not just the ones that tend to spring naturally from certain types of personalities.

Okay, now I'm getting tired just writing these words. How are we to grow *clusters* of God's fruit? Some days the best I seem to be able to offer is a craisin response. It's all I can muster in the edgy atmosphere of my kitchen. More than a craisin is more than I can manage.

We need to remember that it's not about what we can muster and manage. Spiritual fruit grows in our lives by God's initiative as we cooperate with him. It's not up to us to grow all the fruit all at once all the time. But we can cooperate by recognizing where we're missing a fruit that God would like to exhibit in our lives and intentionally asking him to produce it in us.

Let's go back to peace. Nada. Not there. Peace is resting in God in all circumstances. You're doing okay at this fruit when things in life are not irritating or upsetting, but today, well, life is anything but. Your mom just called, and she can't babysit today because she has to go to the doctor. She has found a lump in her breast. Between your own schedule mishap and eruptions of terror and concern for your mom, your heart is as unruly as a bucking bronco on the plains of Wyoming. Peace? Well, that's supposed to be resting in God, right? You can't even sit. Other fruits show up. Love is there . . . in everything. It's thick about you. Self-control appears, its healthy-mindedness holding you back from a moment of Monster Mom rage. But peace? Nope. Nada.

A quantity check reveals where fruit is missing; when we see the absence of fruit, we can ask God to make it present

> A quantity check reveals where fruit is missing; when we see the absence of fruit, we can ask God to make it present by his doing.

by his doing. May sound too simple, but it really is that easy. When we recognize that we don't have a certain fruit in our lives, our only job is to ask God for help. Pause. Say a quick prayer. Remember, it's not all up to you. Cooperate with the Gardener. It's his job to bring the growth.

Quality and quantity are the measurements we can use to evaluate the produce sections of our lives. So how's it growing?

Fruit for Thought

1. Love. Joy. Peace. Patience. Kindness. Goodness. Faithfulness. Gentleness. Self-control. Each one of us more naturally exhibits some of these qualities while missing others. When we don't "get" a certain fruit, we tend to manufacture it ourselves. Look through the list of spiritual fruit for the presence of plastic replacements. Name them. What does the plastic version look like in your personality? How does it

show itself in interactions with your children? With your friends? With your husband?

2. What about the quantity question? Are certain fruits simply absent in your days? Not just plastic replacements but absent altogether? Name them. Now revisit the chapters of these fruits for an update on how you can allow God to grow them in your life.

> *Dear Jesus,*
>
> *Thank you for helping me to see where I struggle with fruit production, both by settling for the plastic stuff and by ignoring the need for several varieties altogether. I recognize the absence of _____ and _____ in my life, and I acknowledge that I can't produce these fruits by myself. They are a result of your work in me. So I invite you to grow them in me!*
>
> *In your name, amen.*

Do not think of yourself more highly than you ought, but rather think of yourself with sober judgment, in accordance with the measure of faith God has given you.

Romans 12:3

fifteen

seasonal fruit

*how do we grow fruit
in all seasons?*

There are times when fruit seems to effortlessly fall from the trees of our lives. Abundant. Lush. Everywhere. Ever-present.

You've experienced such seasons; I have too. Like the season of my father's death. Even though I was busy with young children and my responsibilities at MOPS International and my father lived two thousand miles away from me, somehow life *worked* to allow me to be where I needed to be with a fruit-filled attitude. I remember helping with homework, sans Monster Mom moments, making sack lunches, turning in a report for the office, climbing on a plane that arrived on time, and sitting prayerfully by my father's bedside all in the space of a single day. It wasn't exactly easy. I was sad and concerned. But through it all, I experienced a peace of being able to rest in God, a joy arising from the confidence that he was present even in those difficult days, and patience with all kinds of people and their bumpiness. Fruit grew in my life and from my life and offered sustenance to those around me.

I've also seen such a season in the lives of each of my children. Again, fruit-filled seasons aren't the norm necessarily, but when I look back over the years, certain moments stand out for their undeniable fruitiness.

Like the time when my son, Ethan, was about five and he hollered down the hall to me one night after I'd put him to bed. I returned to his room to find him sitting cross-legged in his upper bunk, bare little chest poking out of his plaid boxers, his blonde hair tousled from sleeplessness.

"Mom, I need to tell you something," he began.

"Okay, Bud, go ahead," I responded.

"Well, it's really hard to get out."

I noticed red blotches growing across his chest. His eyes bore into mine. "Well, Eth, honey, take a deep breath and get it out. It'll be okay," I reassured.

"But Mom, this is BIG!"

Now I was beginning to wonder just what my little treasure of a son had been up to. What on earth did he need to get off his chest so desperately? I took his hands in mine and modeled the deep breath thing, saying, "Take a deep breath, Ethan; it'll be okay."

Ethan's eyes locked on mine as he opened his mouth, sucked in air, paused, and then sang from his toes, "You are so beautiful to me! You are so beautiful to me! You're everything I hoped for; you're everything I need. You are so beautiful-to-me." He sped through the remaining words, pleased with his divulgence. He paused, looked down and then back up, and smiled at me.

I stood, stunned, with Ethan's hands in mine, amazed at this fruit bursting forth from his life. Whoa! Wasn't this every mother's dream? Seeing the fruit of the Spirit produced in her child's life—and toward me, the mom? Love . . . beautiful, there . . . in everything. Love!

Yes, there are such incredible moments, months, even seasons when fruit seems to pop out and plop into the laps of our lives and the lives of those we love.

And then there are other moments when nothing seems to bud. The branches of our days are bare. If juice was flowing through our trunks, we wouldn't know it. We plant ourselves in a relationship with God and wait. When will I look more like love, joy, peace, patience, and less like . . . well, like me? I wake. I work. I wash. I worry. And I look pretty unfruity by the day's end. When will the fruit that makes God visible in me grow? We wonder.

Not seeing much in our own lives, we look to the lives of our children. When will the seeds planted in our children grow such fruit in them? There's the struggle in toddlerhood when every toy is sacred and none can be shared with a playmate. Mercy. Then we watch our kindergartener develop compassion for a friend whose daddy is sick. How precious! However, when we offer this kindness to his own chicken-pox-infested little brother, no more Mister Nice Guy. Instead, he whines over why he can't hold the remote control, why he can't sit on Mommy's lap, and why he has to have soup instead of mac and cheese. Later, in the middle school years, just as we catch a glimpse of what might become fruit, it pops out all scraggly, looking very much like a weed instead of the much-hoped-for fruit. Those "You are so beautiful" moments metamorphose into "You are so nuts" mumblings!

There are stagnant seasons when the production of fruit in our lives and in the lives of those we love is invisible to us. In nature, this quiet stage in which not much seems to happen is called dormancy. In winter, look out your window at the bare-branched trees, or if you live in the desert, the flowerless cacti. Not much seems to be happening in dormancy.

Dormancy increases the yield of a tree—but only by quieting it first.

In some cases, dormancy is a response to external conditions. Growth and fruit production slow due to too much cold, not enough water, and the need for more sun. Similarly, when we encounter external stress, fruit production in our days may slow as well. Joy seems less present. Patience? Well, when we're attacked from the outside, it evaporates. Dormancy stills the production of fruit in our lives due to external issues, but the work of growth continues beneath the surface, and when conditions improve, fruit returns.

> God's job is to grow fruit in our lives. Our job is to be in relationship to him.

How do we grow fruit in *all* seasons—productive and stagnant?

There's an image in the Bible that helps here. It comes from a passage in the Old Testament where the prophet Jeremiah is speaking to the nation of Israel about their need to depend on God to grow them. Sound familiar?

"Blessed is the [one] who trusts in the LORD, whose confidence is in him. [She] will be like a tree planted by the water that sends out its roots by the stream. It does not fear when heat comes; its leaves are always green. It has no worries in a year of drought and never fails to bear fruit" (Jer. 17:7–8).

See how the tree is dependent on the stream, day in and day out, season to season? Because of such a relationship, it grows fruit eventually regardless of its immediate condition. God's job is to grow fruit in our lives in all seasons. Our job is to be in a relationship with him, like a tree is in relationship with streams of water.

What does it mean to be in such a relationship? Two simple actions emerge from this metaphor.

Trees are planted. Being in a relationship with God means making a decision to plant yourself in a connected place with him. We talked about this at the very beginning of this book. The fruit of the Spirit only grows when we are connected with God in a relationship with his Son, Jesus. If this is a step you've skipped, skip no more. Go directly to the Fruit for Thought section at the end of this chapter and walk your way through what it means to be planted in a relationship with God.

Trees send out their roots by the stream. The difference between a bush and a tree is the root system. Bushes blow away because they possess no support system. Trees bear fruit in all seasons because they draw ongoing sustenance from a source of strength beyond themselves. The phrase "sends out its roots by the stream" implies that we hold on to God for our support, for our hope, and for our energy. Practically, we put down the roots

> Trees bear fruit in all seasons because they draw ongoing sustenance from a source of strength beyond themselves.

into God for how we define ourselves as women, for the goals we set as moms and wives, and for the difference our lives will make in this world. Pick up a Bible and read more about the life of Jesus. Take fifteen minutes at the beginning of your day to sit quietly and think through how the Gardener wants to grow his fruit in you and how you can cooperate with him through the items you set down in your day-timer. Ask a friend if she wants to join you in this journey, and then set a time to meet together to talk about how it's "growing."

In season and out, fruit grows when we, like trees, plant ourselves by streams of water.

To grow a life that matters is to produce a fruit-filled life. In season and out, fruit grows when we, like trees, plant ourselves by streams of water. Send down your roots even in the dormant days, and you'll see fruit coming in the future.

Fruit for Thought

1. Perhaps the concept of becoming a tree planted by streams of water in a relationship with God is unfa-

miliar to you. Is this something you'd like to do? Do you want to send your roots into God, depending newly on him to produce his character in you? This simple prayer will help you begin a relationship: "Dear Jesus, I want to plant myself in a relationship with you, like a tree planted by streams of water that sends its roots out by the stream. Every day I want to depend on you to grow the fruit of your character in my life. I know that is what will produce a life that matters. In your name, amen."

2. Are you in a season of obvious fruit production? Look about your days for evidence of fruit. Where do you see fruit growing in your children? How about in you as a woman? How about in your relationship with others who've been hard for you to love? Take heart! Noticing these fruitful and productive moments in life fuels us to face less productive times.

3. If you step back from the dormant trees in your life, can you imagine what is happening beneath the surface, based on the principles of this book? How can you apply the principles of God's job and our job in the growing process to the stage of dormancy?

4. Think through past dormant seasons in your life. Can you give an example of fruit that grew from what seemed like only a barren, lifeless tree? How does such evidence of fruit in past seasons help you endure the dormant seasons of today?

> *Dear Jesus,*
>
> *Help me to understand your perspective on time and growth. When I look at dormant trees in my life, help me to see beyond the barrenness to what you are growing there. Give me restraint so that I don't uproot the trees that are planted and therefore interrupt your work!*
>
> *In your name, amen.*

There is a time for everything, and a season for every activity under heaven . . . a time to plant and a time to uproot. . . . He has made everything beautiful in its time.

Ecclesiastes 3:1, 2, 11

sixteen

fresh fruit

how can we offer fruit to others?

We want our lives to matter—especially we want our relationships with others to affect them for good. And so each day we face a choice: to invest fruitfully or to ignore the opportunity before us. What will you choose?

The choice begins with the opening of my eyes. What will I do today? No, who will I be?

The choice. The decision. The direction of my heart starts with my first conscious thought. I want to grow a life that matters. In me. In my family. In my work. In the relationships that extend outward from me like rings around a pebble plopped into a pond. I want my life to have something to show for it. I want to leave a legacy.

The choice begins with the opening of my eyes, and I continue choosing as I push back the covers, place my feet on the carpet, and head toward the shower and the needs both within and without the walls of my home. It is a clear choice but also costly. I am tired. There are many distractions. But still, I choose.

Today my life will be one of fresh fruit. I choose to co-operate with the Gardener as he sets about growing the fruit of his Spirit in my life. I choose to be planted like a tree by streams of water. I send out my roots by the stream. I invite God into who I am to make me who he always had in mind that I might become: more like Jesus. God made me to reflect his character in my personality. Today I invite God into my moments that he might continue to grow in me.

> I choose to cooperate with the Gardener as he sets about growing the fruit of his Spirit in my life.

In spite of circumstances, I will keep perspective on how fruit grows. There will be cycles of abundance as well as dormant days, but time will round the corner to results as I wait well and live full. Eventually, my life will produce fruit in all seasons, and from the orchards of my days, others will find fresh fruit for their lives as well.

That's what I choose: a fruit-filled life. A life that matters.

And so each day, I rise, freshly seeking fruit. Some mornings I feel sucked dry, a juice box with no juice left. I mentally flip through these amazing qualities—fruit that is naked and pure and cleanly expressed. My tongue salivates. I want them. Love. Joy. Peace. Patience. Kindness. Goodness. Faithfulness. Gentleness. Self-control.

- I will love. I will make a committed choice to be there . . . in everything.
- I will exhibit joy. I will have confidence in God, no matter what happens.

> Eventually, my life will produce fruit in all seasons, and from the orchards of my days, others will find fresh fruit for their lives as well.

- I will practice peace. I will rest in God, knowing that God holds me in the storms of life.

- I will reach for patience. I will hang in there with hard-to-love people.

- I will express kindness. I will meet needs nicely.

- I will model goodness. I will try to be like God, inside and out.

- I will keep faithfulness. I will be true to God.

- I will live gentleness. I will yield myself to God's desires.

- I will choose self-control. I will depend on healthy-minded thinking for all the areas of my life.

Impossible?

No. I will resist the temptation to think all this impossible, even though I fail just minutes into my day. I understand that growing such fruit in my life is not all up to me. My job is to cooperate with God as he grows them. It's up to me to want this fruit-filled life, a life that matters, and to say so to God over and over and over again. It's up to him to grow these qualities in me and then, through me, to show them to others who also want them.

I will offer fresh fruit to my children. I will model the process of cooperating with the Gardener, not hiding all my struggles but allowing my children to watch because I know there are lessons in my failures as well as in my successes. I will recognize the moments of abundant fruit production when all that I've prayed for them occurs in a fabulous harvest season. In the dormant seasons of their days, I will serve as a historian, recalling those prior productions. I will believe that they will experience fruit again when it is difficult for them to believe for themselves.

I will offer fresh fruit to my husband. I will model my yieldedness to the Gardener. I will remain strong in who I am and yet soften as I understand my husband's needs. I will be intentional about exhibiting the freshest of God's fruits to the most familiar of my relationships: my marriage. When it is tempting to settle, to give what is not best but rather what is left over from other efforts, I will hold myself to giving from the "firstfruits" of my energies to the one I have pledged to love above all others.

I will offer fresh fruit to my parents. While they may not have made this offering to me as a child growing up, I will choose to extend these qualities to them. While they may not share my faith or my relationship with God, I will not reject their journeys. I will value the investment they have made in me and will reciprocate the love they have always intended to give me.

I will offer fresh fruit to my friends, my co-workers, and all those I meet in my journey. When I experience the temptation to measure out fruit to this person and not to that one, I will hold myself accountable to the quality and quantity principles of fruit inspection. I will offer all the fruit to all I meet, allowing them to choose according to their wants and wishes. When I am abused in life, I will choose forgiveness and make myself wise with my intentions, but I will continue to offer fruit.

I choose to grow a life that matters. I choose to offer fresh fruit to those around me by seeking it for myself and then by modeling its production in my life day in and day out. My life won't be "perfect." I won't do it "right" all the time. I won't always look "nice" the way others think I should. But in the end, I pray that it can be said about me, "She looks like Jesus."

Fruit for Thought

1. This chapter presents the reality of choice—considered and enacted each day. Look back over the bullets on pages 163–164. Are these your choices? If so, copy and post these words on your bathroom mirror or tuck them in your wallet or in your Bible—somewhere to remind you often of your choosing.

2. Name five realities that get in the way of your choice-making (such as time, busyness, distraction, weariness). How can you eliminate such issues to stay focused on fruit production?

3. Think back to chapter 11 on faithfulness. Just as the Gardener is faithful to produce this fruit in our lives, he is faithful to produce all fruit of the Spirit. How can you use the image of "keeping your appointment" in the orchard to choose fruit day in and day out?

> *Dear Jesus,*
>
> *I choose to cooperate with God as he produces his naked fruit in me. I want to grow and direct my eyes*

toward the goal of my growing: a life that matters
because I possess qualities that look like you.
  In your name, amen.

We know that when he appears, we shall be like him,
for we shall see him as he is.

1 John 3:2

Elisa Morgan is president and CEO of MOPS International, Inc. (www.mops.org), based in Denver, Colorado. Her daily radio program, *MomSense*, is broadcast on more than 700 outlets nationwide. She is the author of *Mom to Mom* and *Meditations for Mothers*, editor of *Mom's Devotional Bible*, and coauthor of *What Every Child Needs, What Every Mom Needs, Children Change a Marriage, Make Room for Daddy*, and *Real Moms*. Morgan lives with her family in Centennial, Colorado.

the MOPS story

You take care of your children, Mom. Who takes care
of you? MOPS International (Mothers of Preschoolers)
provides mothers of preschoolers with the nurture and
resources they need to be the best moms they can be.

MOPS is dedicated to the message that "mothering matters" and that moms of young children need encouragement during these critical and formative years. Groups
meet in more than 3,200 churches and Christian ministries
throughout the United States and in 22 other countries.
Each MOPS program helps mothers find friendship and
acceptance, provides opportunities for women to develop
and practice leadership skills in the group, and promotes
spiritual growth. MOPS groups are chartered ministries
of local churches and meet at a variety of times and loca-
tions: daytime, evenings, and on weekends; in churches,
homes, and workplaces.

The MOPPETS program offers a loving learning experience for children while their moms attend MOPS. Other MOPS resources include *MOMSense* magazine and radio, the MOPS International website, and books and resources available through the MOPShop.

With 14.3 million mothers of preschoolers in the United States alone, many moms can't attend a local MOPS group. These moms still need the support that MOPS International can offer. For a small registration fee, any mother of preschoolers can join the MOPS-to-Mom Connection and receive *MOMSense* magazine six times a year, a weekly Mom-E-mail message of encouragement, and other valuable benefits.

Find out how MOPS International can help you become part of the MOPS-to-Mom Connection and/or join or start a MOPS group. Visit our website at www.mops.org. Phone us at 303-733-5353. Or email Info@mops.org. To learn how to start a MOPS group, call 1-888-910-MOPS.